To ...

From one bad-ass babe to another. You show such strength in your vulnerability. _Thank you_ for the important work you do.

Lucy Lemay Cellucci

You Are Here

Lucy Lemay Cellucci

You Are Here
Published in the United States of America
Copyright 2019 by Lucy Lemay Cellucci
ISBN: 978-1701907447

All rights reserved. No part of this work is transferrable, either in whole or in part. As a purchaser or otherwise lawful recipient of this book, you have the right to enjoy this work in paperback, on your own computer, or another device. Otherwise, it may not be reproduced, stored in a retrieval system, or transmitted in any form or by any means, electronic, mechanical photocopying, recording, or otherwise, without the express prior written permission of both the copyright owner and this publisher. The only exception is brief quotations in printed reviews. Scanning, uploading, and distribution of this book via any means whatsoever are illegal and punishable by law.

This is a work of fiction in that the author created the text. Except for historical and famous characters, all characters, names, places, and events appearing in this work are a product of the author's imagination or used with the permission of the person named. Any resemblance to other real persons, living or dead, is entirely coincidental.

DEDICATION

To my husband, Vittorio. We have spent the last two decades helping each other to become grown-ups. I am thankful for you every day. Also, you make really good coffee.

To my children, Jayden and Olivia. You are the binary star system in my sky. I am forever in awe of the light you create.

ACKNOWLEDGMENTS

Venturing into the unknown wilderness of self-publishing was no easy sprint. It was a marathon of endurance, courage, resourcefulness, and determination. This is one race in which I relied heavily upon my teammates. I would not have seen the finish line if not for the posse of people cheering me on and rehydrating my writer's spirit along the way.

Joleene Moody, you were the firm and encouraging nudge I needed to get my ass in gear and make me see the value of sharing my story. Without you, this book would not exist. I wish for every artist a mentor like you. I look forward to that Vermont ski date in the future. There will be plenty of wine involved. Nuff said.

Gabi Plum, your keen insights and insistence of order and flow are what elevated the quality of my writing. You were the first and last eyes on my book. I am so grateful I had your talents and experience to drawn from. You are a wise and gentle soul with many gifts to offer the world.

Allister Thompson, you have been fixing my grammar and making me look good in print for a full decade now. Your talents have helped to open doors for me while you lead by example of what an indie artist can accomplish with some dedication to their craft. I appreciate having you in my corner.

Vickie Sanford, your expertise in making the formatting for kindle process easy-peasy for me was an invaluable experience. You completely took the stress out of this part. Thank you.

Marie Van Dusen, most people talk about their guardian angels arriving to help them dressed in long, flowing white robes. MY guardian angel arrived wearing a tank top, exposing her ripped biceps! A body-building coach with a background in journalism, you were the perfect motivator to keep me accountable to my goals. I am so grateful for your presence and willingness to provide me with your unfiltered feedback on my writing. I credit you with helping me to craft the voice to reach my audience. It was a blast to experience a creative writing/vodka cooler-infused summer intensive workshop with you. You may want to consider adding this service to your business. Just a thought…

The Storyteller's Circle, you guys are my heart, soul, and tribe. To the women who raised their hand all those months ago and chose to listen to me and let me know that they also experienced similar circumstances in their lives…I say thank you. It is because of you that I had the courage to continue writing on the tough days. A special mention goes out to the following people from the Storyteller's Circle who read sample chapters, shared my writing and sent little notes of encouragement along the way: Tonya Reynolds-Tessier, Sheri Bailey, Kelley Chambers, Wendy Cullen, Louise Tremblay, Nicola Sutton, Vanessa Lachance, Rose-Anne Constantineau, Erin Winrow, Sophie Reitano and Marie Van Dusen. Your support in these early days has meant the world to me and has been the motivating factor to push me across the finish line. You have my eternal gratitude.

Robert West, your guidance has brought about the clarity of mind that was necessary to write this book. When the water is rough and choppy, I take comfort in the fact that I can point my compass west and steer into a safe and calming harbor. Thank you.

"Love yourself first and everything else falls into place." – Lucille Ball

"To live is the rarest thing in the world. Most people just exist." – Oscar Wilde

Contents

Go Inside -Introduction
Where are you?
What Are You Searching For?
Table for One– Why We Need To Be Alone

Go Outside –
Lessons from Mother Nature
Blue Skies
The Trees Have Wi-Fi
Bloom Where You Are Planted

Adhere to Preserve
Think Like a Coyote
Failure — Make it Epic
For Better or Worse –
An Anthology of Marriage
Euclid's Elements of Interplanetary Marriage

Ode to Envy
The Culture of Comparison
The Alchemy of Romantic Love
Coming Home

Mama Knows Best
The Good Mother
Dear Daughter
A Hat of One's Own

Slow Your Roll
Running on Empty
The Illusion of Productivity
Interview with an Insomniac
The Art of Porching
Coffee Break

Conclusion
The Gift of Presence
You Are Here

You Are Here   Lucy Lemay Cellucci

GO INSIDE

WHERE ARE YOU?

The soul which has no fixed purpose in life is lost; to be everywhere, is to be nowhere.--Michel de Montaigne

You are here. Right now. In this exact moment. You occupy your physical space and create your mindset which dictates your thoughts, emotions, and actions. If you have stumbled across these pages I can only surmise that it has little to do with coincidence. You are unhappy. You wish to be free of the burdens you carry in your heart. You want to reclaim your life as the book suggests.

Happy people aren't usually trying to figure out how to be happy. They're two aisles over in the book store solving a murder mystery, being swept off their feet in a fantasy romance or learning the joy of crocheting finger puppets.

But you are here. You are preoccupied with your discontent, insecurity, anger or sadness. Exhausted from chasing perfection only to discover that the reward is shallow. You have picked up this book for a transformative reason.

Something inside you is calling you to examine a

different way of existing in this world. A way to care for yourself without guilt, not as an occasional indulgence but as a regular necessity.

No book (including this one) has all the answers in life. I do not present you with the holy grail on achieving happiness. What I offer is living in tune with the powerful signals already surrounding you which reveal your heart's desires. Right now you can't hear your heart because you're just too damn busy to listen. You are consumed with your daily grind of career, children, and household. You may be struggling with disconnection in your marriage. You may desperately want to exit a failing relationship. Perhaps you are recovering from a painful separation. There are so many moving parts in the engine of your life. It really isn't as simple as just gearing it down to make time for yourself, or is it?

The ironic part is we invite and cling to the stressors in our lives until they destroy us. How on earth did we go from desiring the things we have to resenting them? I have everything I have ever wanted in life. Why do I feel so unable to enjoy any of it?

These are the questions I asked myself as I sat in my doctor's office one sunny morning. I just didn't have the stamina for my life anymore – kids, work, house, marriage –all of it seemed so difficult. There was no ease, no flow, no happiness. Just a sense of constantly grinding through the life I created.

"You sound completely exhausted," my doctor said after listening to my complaints of racing, scattered thoughts, inability to concentrate, prolonged insomnia, constant digestive upset, extreme irritation with everyone around me and lack of energy. "I think you may be experiencing depression." She said factually.

I sat in that chair and listened as she outlined my options for dealing with what I perceived as an epic, personal failing.

Depression.

I had been resisting that word for a long time. It dripped with failure like a leaky roof onto my head. Depression drenched everything around me, filling buckets in every corner of my house. I felt a saturating inadequacy as I quietly accepted I was unable to function the way I used to and manage my life as an adult.

"Have you ever thought about harming yourself?" my doctor asked me, trying to gauge how far down the rabbit hole I'd fallen. I stared at a piece of fluff on the carpet as I spoke. "Sometimes I think about driving my car off a bridge," I confessed. "What stops you from carrying through?" she asked. "Well, to be honest with you, I don't think I'd be able to fit it into my schedule. There isn't a lot of time in my week for me to be able to pull off something like that."

I looked up from the carpet and met her eyes. She tried to speak but all that came out was a sharp snort. She put her hand over her mouth. She was trying not to laugh.

I was confused. Wait…what were we talking about again? I suddenly worried I may have shared an inappropriate story involving a herd of sheep, a jug of plum wine and a druid priest who was feeling unusually frisky. No, it wasn't that. I promised myself I'd never repeat that story.

She was laughing at me, perhaps more accurately, with me. Here we sat, giggling away at the idea of me being too busy to orchestrate a proper suicide. The absurdity of the situation was suddenly hilarious.

"Please, forgive me," she said a moment later. "I've never heard anyone describe it that way before. I know exactly what you mean. Most days I have appointments scheduled so tightly I hardly use the bathroom. I don't even take a proper lunch break. Most of my colleagues work this way. Then we go home and it's all about driving the kids to activities and homework…it is terrible what we do to ourselves."

I looked at her with a startling revelation. I had something in common with my doctor. My exhausted, failure-to-adult-ass had something in common with this accomplished medical professional. Could it be I wasn't as much of a screw-up as I thought? This was my first clue something bigger was at work here.

I left my doctor's office with a prescription for

anti-depressants. I felt incredibly deflated for needing medication to cope with my life. She explained to me if I was a diabetic I'd take medication to manage that problem. This was no different. Fair enough. I could buy into that reasoning. I am not a nay-sayer for the use of pharmaceuticals to treat depression. We need to get over our hang-ups and embrace individual courses of treatment that work for us.

But these pills were not my answer.

Three weeks later I returned to my doctor. The medication had swiftly dealt with the insomnia but now I felt I was hovering between unconsciousness and the first twenty seconds of waking up. The feelings of sadness or being at my wits end had disappeared but so did everything else. Now I just felt nothing. I was so sedated I could calmly look at the drapes for an entire afternoon. I was the love child of Flat Stanley and Eeyore from Winnie-the-Pooh.

My doctor agreed it would be best to stop the medication and seek out a qualified therapist instead. I offered no resistance. I would do anything to feel human again.

After a few weeks of therapy, my worst fears were confirmed: my problems were indeed all in my head. I was a chronic over-thinking, over-extended and overwhelmed person. My negative thoughts and self-limiting beliefs were patterns I learned over time. The good news? If I thought myself into this mess I also had the power to think my way out of it.

This was my first and most important step to getting where I am today.

This is my new *here*.

This can be your *here*.

This book can be digested in a few short sittings. If you can give yourself that time, I can show you how to build a bridge from where you are now to where you want to be. All you require is a willingness for self-examination and time to reflect on where you want to be in your life, here and now.

Let's begin…

WHAT ARE YOU SEARCHING FOR?

"There is a misconception of those who explore; it is not answers they seek, but the longing for another question."—Brian S Woods
The Codex Bellum III: The Observer Effect

You are holding a collection of stories that were forged from the molten lava of suffering. The body that carried this great pain was completely disconnected from its heart. If you were to see the face that accompanied this body, you would be completely unaware of the underlying turmoil as it usually reverted to the factory default setting of a smile. Appearing happy to others while quietly simmering in discontent is a sleight of hand that we women master within our tenures of domesticity. If, somewhere inside, you have experienced a quiet, yet unshakable acknowledgment of this unsettling truth then I urge you to keep reading.

In an age where the grand preoccupation with online media and the crafting of social images has become our norm, we have elevated seeking outside of ourselves from a survival skill to an epidemic of personal proportions. Though we've acquired food, shelter, the ability to make fire on demand, mating partners, offspring, careers, and hobbies, we are still looking outward in search of something to anesthetize the quiet hum of dissatisfaction that lies beneath our perfectly filtered Instagram pictures and cleverly crafted hashtag comments. This begs the question: if we're so good at *#winningatlife* online, why are so many of us failing to be *genuinely happy* offline? The answers we seek cannot be found until we look in the one place we've discounted from the beginning: *inside ourselves.* True joy: that enviable state-of-being where young children and the newly-in-love appear to reside is available in abundance to each and every one of us who know how to create and cultivate it in our day-to-day lives.

IS RESTLESSNESS PART OF OUR DNA?

Humans have always been seekers. We have journeyed far and wide in search of food, shelter, potential mating partners and eventually, education and career opportunities. Now we can add *purpose* to the list. Why are we here? What are we meant to do? What makes us happy? By design, human evolution has trained us to look outside of ourselves to survive. If our ancestors had never explored their environments, they would not have found shelter. If they had never left their caves, they would have starved. If they hadn't sought out a mate, our species would not have survived. Humans learned early on that in order to survive, they would have to constantly look outside themselves to meet their needs.

Fast-forward a few million years to modern-day society and we're still turning to outward sources to get our needs met. Our smartphones, on-line shopping accounts, Fitbits, social media, and adrenaline-producing hobbies are the go-to for many of us trying to fill the void. When they stop working we move on to something else. At what point do we finally feel fulfilled?

WHAT'S THE TIPPING POINT?

These pages come on the heels of a morning that began with typical domestic misery: kids waking up too early, making too many demands before the first cup of caffeine, a messy house screaming for the kind of attention that I cannot bring myself to give it, a disappointing balance in the family bank account and the familiar, grumpy silence between two people who have worked tirelessly to create a life that at times leaves them wanting nothing more than to flee from it.

What set this morning apart from so many others was my resolve to stop pushing against it and simply take a break. For several hours I walked the paths of a nearby conservation area. I marveled at the trees, birds and the reflection of the sky in the water. I relished the silence of my solitude. I didn't have anybody making any demands of me and I didn't have to speak to anyone either. I wasn't a referee, a cook, nor a social director. I didn't have to sign any permission forms or help anybody find their damn socks. I wasn't fulfilling any of my usual roles: wife, mother, dance teacher, nor as of late, unmotivated, procrastinating writer. I was an anonymous person who was simply enjoying a lovely morning walking by the river. Bit by bit, that tight knot inside my chest started to unravel. My thoughts began to wander in that slow, meandering way parenthood seldom allows yet artistry frequently craves. As my eyes panned across the river to other side of the bank, something released inside. I felt my shoulders detach themselves from my ears. A warm feeling spread inside my chest. I recognized it immediately: happiness. *Where the hell have you been?*

Of course, that blissful, peaceful feeling has been there all along; I'd been too distracted to notice. My focus has been directed toward grocery shopping, meal planning, soccer games, swimming lessons, dental appointments, and work responsibilities. First world priorities always demanding my immediate attention. Once again I had allowed myself to be drawn and quartered by distraction, slicing through me like a dagger, fragmenting my spirit into pieces that are too small and weak to feel the joy that stems from simply being alive. Just then another anomaly occurred. Inspiration wound itself around me like a snake coiling around a branch. I was struck by the urge to create; something that had not occurred in quite some time. It was here on this wooden boardwalk by the river's edge that I decided the time had come for me to resume the creative life.

This book is the result of a summer spent reconnecting with me through the practice of weekly (and eventually, daily) solitude. Over several mornings I visited many of the local conservation areas that surround my Ottawa, Ontario home. During these quiet moments of reprieve, the idea for this book came to me. My intention with these pages is twofold: first and foremost, I want to make it clear to you, lovely lady, that you are not alone in your experiences of being overwhelmed, overextended, and under-fulfilled. If your love for your family and all the roles you take on has you wanting to explode with joy one minute and then ready to execute an escape plan that requires a fake ID, a one-way plane ticket and a bottle of bleach the next, then this book is for you.

Second, I'd like to help you by gently redirecting your focus from the places where you feel there is a lack and reclaim your power by showing you that it is possible to make yourself happy in a sustainable and authentic way, without the use of opioids, an illicit affair, or an entire housekeeping staff.

I have observed several universal themes of human

suffering through my own experiences as well as those of others. We are prone to depression, anxiety, and exhaustion. We fall prey to crises of identity, health, and marital dissatisfaction. It is for women during the season of midlife that these themes reach their tipping point.

IS IT ME OR THEM?

Perhaps you have noticed that a sense of unease has settled within you. It was once no bigger than the seed of a dandelion but quietly and unsuspectingly it has taken root and grown heavy with burdensome thought. These ruminations may manifest in a variety of ways: growing resentment and irritation with loved ones, feelings of being tethered to your life rather than living it, marital discord, vocational dissatisfaction or perhaps a sense of searching for a higher purpose beyond feeding people and paying bills. These are the troubling preoccupations of one who is searching for the answers to difficult questions. Often, the impulse is to silence those uncomfortable feelings to one degree or another with a distraction. We pour the wine, host the book clubs, endlessly throw our hat in the volunteer ring, take on back-to-back renovation projects, or start rekindling old flames on Facebook. For a time there is relief, but the reprieve is short-lived. We may be living in modern times but matters of a restless heart are timeless in their nature. One only has to look upon the work of the late nineteenth-century German poet, Rainer Maria Rilke, to see we are repeating the many versions of discontentment in modern times.

"Be patient toward all that is unsolved in your heart and try to love the questions themselves, like locked rooms and like books that are now written in a very foreign tongue. Do not now seek the answers, which cannot be given you because you would not be able to live them. And the point is, to live everything. Live the questions now. Perhaps you will then gradually, without noticing it, live along some distant day into the answer."

In my twenties, I attempted to read and comprehend Rilke. I read *Letters to a Young Poet* and was entirely underwhelmed. Frustrated by a lack of conclusion or truth, I tossed aside my copy of this brilliant novella and proclaimed it quackery and gobbledygook. Twenty-some-odd years later, I see the error of my ways and have come to regard this man as a poetic genius.

The above passage, in particular, brings me comfort in the way that it gives me permission to stop fretting madly over the discord that has crept into my life over the years. Restlessness, unease, discomfort —these are the hallmarks of personal growth. These feelings, as unsettling as they may be, are a calling for us to evolve into a better, more compassionate version of ourselves. It is the shedding of an older, more constricted skin that no longer serves us. To resist these feelings, to push them away rather than be open to what they are showing us, is akin to ripping open a cocoon to rescue a caterpillar from becoming a butterfly and growing its wings.

LET'S PAUSE TOGETHER

Throughout each section of the book, we will uncover the joy that is ever-present in life when we turn away from the business of doing and focus instead on the business of being. My hope is that our time together in these pages will provide a sojourn from your own distractions. My goal is to inspire you to find your own way to reconnect with joy and rediscover the woman who stares back at you in the mirror, desperately waiting to be seen.

So go and brew yourself a cup of your favorite tea, wrap yourself in something warm and fuzzy, and let me give you a place to rest that tired and weary head of yours. It's time to replenish your reserves so that you too can see that despite whatever circumstance you find yourself in, true happiness is your choice to make every day.

Now let me tell you a story.

TABLE FOR ONE
WHY WE NEED TO BE ALONE

"Loneliness is the poverty of self. Solitude is the richness of self."—
May Sarton

"Will anyone be joining you?" the waitress asked as she handed me my menu.

"No," I answered cheerfully, relishing the shady little corner of the outdoor patio where I had chosen to stop and eat lunch that day. "I'm alone."

Since the time I set myself to gathering ideas to form this book, I have begun the process of regularly practicing solitude. At first, it was just in the evenings seated on my porch. I held court on a wooden chair surrounded by the flowers and shrubs I had planted in the front garden years before. In these early days of my practice I would race around all day long taking comfort in the knowledge that the last hour of the day was solely mine; sitting on my porch, greedily squeezing out the last of the fading orange light from the sky like a crushed tangerine between my eager palms.

During those hours of quiet contemplation I slowly eased into an openness I had previously denied myself. The constant mental chatter began to quiet, the impulse to always be *doing* began to settle, and a deep-seated feeling of peace started growing from within. I started watching the neighbors across the street. The couple were building an immaculate garden. As I watched them toil the evening hours away removing sod, digging, planting, mulching and watering, I noticed the feelings that surfaced.

At first, there was admiration for how hard they were working. This was soon followed by discomfort. I realized that in sitting there observing their project take shape I was not working hard at all.

I mean, look at these two champs knocking it out of the park! One of them has just spent a full day working at an office while the other has been caring for two small children, but here they are throwing more dirt around than Us Weekly.

Honestly, did I not have several home improvement projects of my own that required my attention? My kitchen cupboards needed to be reorganized. My refrigerator had a science experiment underway in the vegetable crisper. Somewhere was a scrapbook for my daughter's baby years that I still hadn't started (she was in grade school by this point), a bedroom that was seriously in need of some redecorating and a garage that was about to spew its contents across the driveway the next time a child went in to grab their bike. Who the hell was I to just *sit there and watch?* The impulse to get up and get to work on a task of my own was strong and pervasive. My right leg started to shake a little. My foot was tapping lightly to the beat of its own rhythm on the underlying concrete. *Lazy-lazy-watch-them-work-you're-a-good-for-nothing-jerk.*

But I was determined. I kept my behind in that chair. I consumed an entire cup of tea while it was still hot. I observed the barrage of verbal insults that were coming at me from within. I allowed myself to feel compassion for that internal, task-driven workaholic who resides in me and has garnered praise from the outside world for being so damn efficient. In that moment I felt sorry for her and how exhaustion was preventing her from enjoying so much in life. I decided she would get a break that evening and under no circumstance would she be permitted to leave the porch and weed the vegetable garden.

Once I accepted my fate as a hostage of relaxation another unsettling feeling took root. My neighbor's garden was huge, spanning their entire front lawn, while my own addition of greenery was limited to a hydrangea bush, a handful of Hostas, and a few lousy irises. Now I had switched gears from anxiety to envy. How beautiful their front lawn was! The curb appeal! The added value to their property! I should do the same. At the very least, it would bring me joy to sit in the beauty of a fully landscaped front lawn.

But no. Onward, I sat. Nothing, I did. Stillness, I embodied.

Not only did I stay the course of quiet, contemplative inactivity but now I was also talking backward. Master Yoda would be proud. As early summer transitioned into late summer, I started noticing how much joy and relaxation I was receiving simply from looking at and appreciating my neighbor's garden. I didn't have to possess the object of beauty to receive joy from it. I only had to hold it as my object of attention. This made me wonder if I'd been going about this whole I-need-to-have-this-and-that-to-be-happy business the wrong way. From a young age, we are trained to be good students of consumerism. We are groomed to think of acquisition as a vehicle to happiness. If this truly were the case, that swimming pool or sports car or vacation home would have done the trick to cure our malaise years ago. No, the answer to finding true contentment does not lie in collecting material objects. Contrary to many pursuits of human satisfaction, the happiest people I have come across are those who choose to live simply.

Feeling the urge to probe these questions a little deeper, I began to increase my moments of solitude. I started getting up a little earlier in the morning to ensure I would have at least thirty minutes before the household came to life. I was able to greet the new day with a sense of quiet appreciation for the many blessings I had been given. I used this time to read the thoughts of history's great thinkers, to write my own contemplations, to pursue my own aspirations. I found all these things went a long way to cultivating feelings of contentment and fulfillment. I began to invest in myself and my emotional well-being. This would not have been possible without the practice of regular solitude.

We give little value to the need for solitude in our society. The world is built for couples and families of four or more. There are numerous dating websites to facilitate meeting your soul mate. Restaurants beg you to bring your children in on Monday nights so they can eat for free, and timeshares boast large discounts to parties of ten or more people. Everywhere you go the message is quantity over quality.

Solitude should be embraced as an essential part of the human experience. Our friendly neighborhood German poet, Rainer Maria Rilke, had explored this concept in depth beyond an intellectual understanding as he widened his hours of solitude to extend beyond what was necessary to compose his literary work.

"But your solitude will be a support and a home for you, even in the midst of very unfamiliar circumstances, and from it, you will find all your paths."

Only from a place of solitude can you truly make space for your authentic self. It is the exterior persona through which we live that creates our drama and suffering. This is especially true for women who are most often the caretakers within the family unit. Caught up in a never-ending cycle of duties and commitments, life takes on the quality of a nomadic caravan as we move about our day from one task to another. We women become an impressive collection of functions. We are on the clock from the moment our eyes open. Can we get it all done?

Sadly, in Western culture, this is the place where the female spirit resides. In the land of *doing*. And in all of the *doing*, the *being* gets neglected.

Women in particular, and I say this only because my gender is notorious for putting themselves last, are in great need of creating a sacred space for themselves. We must guard that space with the tenacity of a thousand lionesses. All of us are in need of time and space to decompress, daydream and recharge. Healing something — whether it be a broken arm or spirit — requires substantial reserves of energy. How many of us were drawn to stories like *Eat, Pray, Love*, or *Wild*, where women went on courageous journeys in the name of growth, healing, and self-discovery? You don't have to wander the Pacific Crest Trail or fly to Italy to eat cheese alone in an apartment to clear your head and find peace in your heart. (Although it certainly wouldn't hurt!) All you need to do is make regular time for yourself and refuse to give it up for anything or anyone.

On a daily basis, it can mean you have some me-myself time at the end of the day with a cup of tea and a book. On a weekly basis, you could block off a couple of hours to go out for lunch by yourself or register yourself for a class of some sort. On a monthly basis, you could take a moonlight yoga class. On a yearly basis, you could insist on a weekend (a whole week would be even better) without family members tagging along. Your choices don't matter as long as you sign yourself up, announce your intentions to your family and continue bringing yourself to your own playdates.

Solitude is your best antidote to counter the turmoil of your life. It can quiet your anxious mind, soothe your restless heart and reconnect your soul with its source. Within the sanctity of solitude, you can train yourself to stop cranking the handle of the venomous thought generator. Solitude can bridge the gap between unity and diversity of spirit. If we do not become vigilant in our efforts to rejuvenate and recharge, we rob ourselves of the ability to take delight in the company of others. People grate on our nerves when bitterness seeps into our hearts, thoughts, and words. We become impatient and unkind toward our loved ones and people in general. We begin to experience a different kind of loneliness. A loneliness that doesn't stem from being alone, but rather leaves you feeling as isolated as a shipwrecked castaway although you're surrounded by friends at social gatherings. When we are unable to connect with ourselves we have no hope of forging meaningful connections with others. To be lonely in the company of others is one of the saddest experiences of the human condition. All paths of overextension lead to isolation. While it seems counterintuitive to use the regular practice of solitude to guard against isolation, this can be achieved through reframing our perspective of what it means to be alone.

When we learn to value our own company we are invited to enjoy a whole new way of being in the world. We begin to understand how to fill our own needs. We can derive pleasure from lunching alone, going to a movie alone or even traveling alone. When we create a space that is uniquely ours to nurture our spirits and cultivate our own passions we are showing the world that we matter. Getting to know yourself and deciding that you are, in fact, pretty cool to hang out with, is a gift, not every woman will give herself. If you cannot bear to be alone with yourself for two hours it speaks volumes of the neglected relationship that exists within yourself.

Often we feel a selfishness in the idea of regularly practicing time away from our families. To those of you who cannot allow the family unit to do without your presence for a few hours each week, I would ask you to imagine watching your daughters stepping into your roles. We pour countless energy and time into our children helping them to cultivate their interests and talents. We do this because we want them to have positive experiences and lead fulfilling lives. We want them to feel joy and be joyful. Why, then, do we not extend the same expression of love to ourselves? If you saw your daughter running around like a headless chicken, caring for everyone but herself, would you say, "Wow! Great work, sweetie. Remember, they all matter more than you."?

If she confessed her exhaustion, would you counsel her to drink wine in the evenings and suggest that she blow off a little steam by crying in the shower or in her car when she was alone? Few of us would ever set the bar for our children's happiness that low yet we continue to do it to ourselves.

In order to remove the rut we have carved out for ourselves, we must treat ourselves with the same level of compassion we would a close friend or loved one. We must give ourselves permission to rest and dream and reach for our desires. Neglecting this creates an angry, exhausted and ineffective person caring for the people we love the most. These are not the seeds we intend to sow as parents, but it happens so gradually we hardly take notice until a breakdown of spirit occurs, and we begin searching for relief in toxic places.

We can refine our idea of being wholly present with ourselves, changing our view of solitary *confinement* to one of solitary *refinement*. In that reframing, we make a beautiful space for life to unfold for us. Life will show you who you are and all that you have the potential to be if you allow it. That's a wonderful feeling to enjoy as you sit with your lunch at a table for one.

GO OUTSIDE

Lessons learned from Mother Nature

BLUE SKIES

~~~

"Before you can change your life for the better, change your thoughts for the better."
—Debasish Mridha

One of the things I enjoy doing most when I am alone is looking at the sky. There is something so calming about gazing into that vast ocean of blue hovering above my head. I love how clear and endless the morning sky appears when it is unblemished with clouds. It stretches out before me, a blank canvas I use to bring shape to my scattered thoughts. Naturally, I begin to consider my past. I am in awe of the fact the sky I look up to in this stage of my life is the same one I used to stare at as a child. One of the things that used to puzzle me was the how the stars would speckle the night sky with a dazzling show of light but disappear out of sight during the day. A few years after I became a parent I was presented with this very question from my own children. I decided that we all deserved an explanation.

The short response to this question is, of course, that the daytime light of our own sun blocks out the light of the more distant stars. But there's more going on up there. What we call *light* is a small portion of the electromagnetic radiation visible to our eyes. Sunlight is made up of the entire light spectrum but nitrogen and oxygen in the Earth's atmosphere permit the color blue to scatter most efficiently.

That blue light is so bright it trumps the light from much farther stars. Those other stars still exist but are not visible with our limited perception. We perceive their absence. Our perception is what creates our reality, so we only see blue.

The same rings true on cloudy days when a blanket of overcast mist obscures my view of that calming blue light. That beautiful blue sky doesn't go anywhere; I just don't see it in that moment. It is here I realize that much of the discord and unrest that percolates within me is also of my own skewed perception. Anyone who is prone to gravitating towards a negative mental outlook or has battled the headless horsemen of depression, anxiety, and other mood-deteriorating conditions has witnessed a beautiful blue sky turn dark and cloudy. Dark and cloudy may present as job loss, financial difficulties, parenting challenges, romantic rejection, failed academic studies, friendship loss, personal humiliation; there is no shortage of disappointing life events where negative feelings may arise. These experiences leave us with a general sense of malaise, prompting us to go away and lick our wounds for a while, indulging in self-pity. Some of us recruit props for these occasions, ranging anywhere from a couple of pints of Hagen Daas to the help of Mr. Jack Daniel. Others select the use of stronger substances for mood elevation.

Substance abuse offers many vices. We can use the physical affections of others as distraction while our neighbors may prefer to soothe themselves with a little retail therapy. Some of us will even physically harm ourselves in an effort to change our focus from the gloomy clouds overhead. As a species, we've evolved many creative ways to distract ourselves from pain. Psychological suffering is often the direct result of projecting past pain into present situations. We have a knack for recycling old hurts into new dramas. Not only do we drag the past around with us, we anxiously obsess about the future as we gaze into our imaginary crystal balls. Our suffering, no matter what the catalyst, is the product of our inability to remain in the present moment. We become hyper-focused on our problems and negativity, thereby inviting more of the same into our lives.

Sinking into this downward spiral creates further isolation as we cut ourselves off from the vital life force residing in all of us. Rather than surrender to the options of depression, distraction, or delusion, we can choose the path that shifts from a state of isolation into a state of connection. When we are fully present and allow ourselves the feeling of connection we no longer experience pain. I have learned to achieve this connection for myself through daily practice of gratitude meditation. Though it may seem counterintuitive to focus on your blessings when you feel a deficit in joy, gratitude is the natural antidote to fear-based emotions like anger, despair, and anxiety.

Studies have concluded meditation effectively moves function away from the brain's limbic system which is connected to emotion, memories, and arousal, into the prefrontal cortex which governs cognitive functioning, personality development, decision-making, behavior, and expression.

During times of low mood, we witness our energy and motivation dry up like a puddle in the desert sand. We can hardly walk up a flight of stairs without summoning the herculean effort required to run a marathon. Thoughts are difficult to articulate, and we may become aloof within our social circles. Nothing seems to generate any measure of enjoyment. All we see are those damn dark clouds stretching across our sky, obscuring the beautiful blue and turning it gray. In these times we feel purposeless and adrift. Weighed down with sadness, guilt, shame, or just plain indifference toward life, we sink into the abyss as swiftly as we jumped fully clothed into the black, swirling waters of a deep river with our pockets full of stones. We question our chosen career paths, our choices in partners, our decisions to start families. Surely our lives would be better if we'd only — wait a minute —does that cloud look like a dragon? It does! A large, scaly, fire-breathing dragon. The outline is so clear! Even the wings are immaculately detailed. It looks like it's trying to … no, I was mistaken. It's not a dragon. It's a wild boar. I can see the sharp angle of the turned-up snout with protruding tusks on each side. Even the dragon's clawed feet (what I thought looked like clawed feet) have morphed into hooves. How could I ever have thought that cloud was a dragon when it's clearly … a car. Yes, that's it. A car. Those aren't hooves. They're tires! And then with just the right amount of wind the car melts away, revealing the empty sky behind it.

    I am looking up, left with nothing but my perception of what I *thought* was going on up there. Those clouds, those thoughts and the restless feelings they stir, are constantly in motion. They change shape and twist around each other in a cerebral dance only I can see. As I watch the dragon and the boar drive away together in their strange little car, I recognize a lesson about handling those gloomy periods when my blue skies are full of dark clouds.

I lower myself into the grass and turn my gaze upward. That blue sky, full to the brim with peace, contentment, and happiness, is still there. I make space for the stormy weather that has blown across. I close my eyes, take several slow, deep breaths and allow the nervous energy I am accustomed to carrying settle and surrender. I observe without judgment what is present inside me. Now, I have made room to invite gratitude into my heart. When I stop focusing on what is painful and put my attention on what is beautiful in my life the shift in my *thinking* results in a shift in my *feelings*.

Each person's clouds have different messages to share. Perhaps yours holler out unlovable, bad parent, failure or goat fornicator (yikes). Cloudy emotions are skilled in assigning labels which elicit strong responses in their intended recipients. Instead of taking in all those hurtful messages, you could let them pass on through. Watch them take shape, acknowledge them as they sail by: *unlovable, bad parent, failure, Hey! Goat fornicator! Up high, man! How y'all doin' today?* Do not buy into what they are selling. Do not take what you hear as a statement of truth. Just like the strange dragon/boar/car cloud, you realize it is simply a matter of perception. Let it continue past until its shape has changed so many times there is nothing left of it to block out the blue sky you thought was permanently lost. Bear witness to those messages, but not ownership.

When I make myself confront my troubles and refuse to accept the propaganda of negative thinking, the weather forecast changes in my favor. Once again, I have my beautiful blue sky filled with the good things I believe are always present in myself. The happiness we seek is always hovering above our heads. The question is, what will we choose to see?

THE TREES HAVE WI-FI

"Look deep into nature, and then you will understand everything better." – Albert Einstein

Since I was a young child, trees have always held a certain fascination for me. If I wasn't climbing their branches or seeking shade under their canopy, I was drawing trees, making art with their leaves or decorating them for holiday celebrations. The backyard of my childhood home had a robust silver maple tree that sadly had to be cut down when I was eleven due to a caterpillar infestation. Though I attempted to stage a protest to save my beloved tree, my efforts were ineffective due to my inability to convince any other children in the neighborhood to join me.

As an adolescent, I won the role of a tree in the cast of our local theater production, *Into the Woods*. Dressed head-to-toe in green tie-dye, I danced and sang and conveyed the emotional consciousness of the forest — it was deep. As an adult, there is nothing more relaxing and grounding for me than being outdoors, surrounded by trees. The summer my family drove from eastern Ontario up through the more remote parts of northern Ontario was a reminder of the regal beauty that lines the corridors of our Canadian highways, like soldiers standing at attention. Watching as the transformation of the tree line took place, the emergence of the stately hardwoods was like following a welcoming trail of breadcrumbs into the cradle of what my heart recognized as home. This summer, spending my time on the paths of the conservation areas in my city, is no different.

I am in good company though. Suzanne Simard, a professor of Forest Ecology at the University of British Columbia holds her own long-time fascination with trees. Simard conducted research and realized her theories about trees communicating with each other through hidden complex social networks.

Using traceable radioactive carbon isotopes and a Geiger counter, Simard measured the transfer of carbon molecules between individual tree species. Her initial studies focused on the relationship between two species, birch, and Douglas fir. Simard's findings suggest these two trees were engaged in "lively conversation" as carbon molecules were actively traded between them depending on what growth cycle the trees were in. Birch trees received extra carbon from Douglas firs when the birch trees were losing their leaves. Douglas firs received extra carbon from birch trees when they were in shaded areas and unable to photosynthesize. The trading post for this commerce of carbon and other nutrients occurred within the root system of the trees beneath the forest floor.

Simard's research also identified the establishment of hub trees or "mother trees." Mother trees are among the oldest and largest of the trees. Mother trees nurture young seedlings sending them their excess carbon and other nutrients that enable them to grow. When mother trees are diseased or dying, they send all of their carbon defense signals and other chemical messages of wisdom to their young. This transfer of sustenance and knowledge results in an increase of resilience to future stressors for the young trees. The hardiness of the whole forest community benefits. Forests, in their natural splendor, have an enormous capacity to self-heal, in much the same way as humans and other animals do. This comparison is not lost on me as I sit in the palm of a gigantic oak, looking out at the Rideau River.

OUR ROLES AS MOTHER TREES TO SUPPORT DIVERSITY

In Simard's opinion, it is important that we develop more holistic and reverent attitudes in our forestry practices. Current models of clear-cutting and replanting only one or two desirable species of trees will create new forests that lack complexity and are vulnerable to infection and infestations. If we deplete our woodlands of too many mother trees we run the risk of having the whole system collapse.

The underground network of the tree community mirrors our own complex human social structure. At our deepest levels, we are invisibly bound, roots entwined with our parents, children, siblings, spouses, friends, neighbors and community. Acting as mother trees, we nurture our young and pass along our own messages of wisdom. We shape future generations of adults and provide the necessary tools to develop their own resilience and self-healing capabilities. Sadly, some families face tragedy in losing their parental figures or *mother trees* too early. Losses may result from physical disease, accidents, mental illness, or addictions. Children affected by this type of loss will be as traumatized as roots in the throes of transplant shock. If not properly healed, the pain of that loss will later be transferred onto their own children along with a legacy of parental pain.

The same applies for communities and nations who lose their leaders at untimely moments, as was the case on April 4th, 1968, when Dr. Martin Luther King, Jr. was assassinated in Memphis, Tennessee. Waves of pain and anger reverberated through several black communities. Their charismatic speaker and Christian leader who had worked to advance civil rights through nonviolent demonstration and civil disobedience was ripped from the world at a time when it needed him the most. Chaos ensued as riots broke out in many American cities.

Like the complex structure of the Canadian boreal forest, our own communities and workplaces also benefit from a diverse population. We are in great need of the mosaics of racial, religious, and gender differences. The communion of give-and-take that occurs when we learn to embrace and celebrate our differences rather than reject and disrespect them is a powerful nutrient boost to the soil in which the human spirit grows. This serves humanity in the most positive of ways. Without celebrating our differences we are vulnerable to social infections. Racial prejudice, misogynistic attitudes, homophobia and a general lack of reverence for life seeps into the soil surrounding our roots. When we devalue people based upon their differences from ourselves we devalue all of human life as a whole. We pass on the messages to children: women have limited value, white skin is better than brown, Indigenous lives don't matter, non-heterosexual orientation is wrong, all people who pray to Allah are terrorists. We cultivate an ugliness that rots the deepest levels of our social network. It chokes out gratitude, compassion and kindness — the good nutrients of humanity and most powerful inoculations we have to fight against hatred.

There are a million ways to extend kindness and gratitude to others: during the month of April, if you live in Canada, you could brush the snow off the car beside you in the parking lot. This is the season we like to call "still freakin' winter." You could put coins in a stranger's parking meter, give a compliment about a server to their manager, visit your lonely neighbor or volunteer your time. Start off simply with the people around you and make it a point to notice and comment on something positive about them every day.

As I climb down the enormous trunk of my viewing perch, I set the intention to live with kindness in my thoughts each new day. I know there will be days when I fall embarrassingly short of my goals. If I keep working toward living with kindness, I have a much better chance of thriving instead of just surviving. Kindness and gratitude are the greatest legacies a person can leave behind. No career or financial success will leave as significant an impact nor inspiration for those around you. To quote the words of Mahatma Gandhi, "You must be the change you want to see in the world." Only then will we be capable of creating the kinds of societies that will stand tall and draw strength from their roots at their invisible connections, just as the majestic trees in our precious forests do, if only we are able to take our cues from the harmonious interactions of the birch and Douglas fir trees by supporting our diversity rather than attacking it.

BLOOM WHERE YOU ARE PLANTED

"Life isn't about waiting for the storm to pass. It's about learning to dance in the rain."
—Vivian Greene

If you are anything like me, spring is a time of year to be greatly preoccupied with all things related to gardening. I have killed as many plants as I have successfully grown. Disclaimer: I could fill an entire season of *How Not to Garden* on HGTV. Because I love growing my own flowers and veggies I persist, despite the carnage I leave behind.

The crown jewel of my garden is a particularly hearty variety of blooming shrub known as the Diablo Ninebark. I love this plant for so many reasons; mostly because I can't kill it. Though it flowers better in full sun it tolerates shade. While its preference is well-drained soil kept evenly moist, it grows in wetland conditions and clay. Now I'll blow your mind further by letting you know it can tolerate drought! The Diablo Ninebark is an adaptive species of plant that does not require ideal conditions to thrive. Unlike the delicate rose which requires the perfect conditions to show its beauty, Diablo has mastered the ability to bloom no matter where it is planted. This makes it akin to a dandelion. That crazy yellow mofo will bust through concrete to open its petals and scream *boo-ya* in your face. For this reason, I consider this plant to be an excellent role model — my mentor if you will — and I've applied its ninja-like adaptability in my own life.

We have tricked ourselves into believing we need ideal conditions in our lives in order to thrive. We feel happiness is waiting for us to find the right relationship, the dream house, lose twenty pounds, snag the promotion, get pregnant, published, recognized, etc.

We press pause on our contentment while we wait for perfection. By keeping our "eyes on the prize," we miss all the good stuff happening around us right now.

We waste a lot of time and energy looking for happy. Especially when it's already inside us. All we have to do is turn the key to unlock its potential and allow it to flow. Not an easy task when you are hung up on having something before feeling happy. If we want to be winners in the game of happiness, we must be willing to reverse engineer it by feeling happy *before* having the things.

"But how can I feel happy when I'm so miserable?" the skeptic inside me once scolded. During these low periods, I focus on what I lack in life. I am infected with the "I don't have enough" virus. This nasty psychological contagion spreads regret, inadequacy, and envy. It leaves its victim suffering from malaise and disempowerment. "I don't have enough" can leave its grimy film on anything in my life. I have felt it seeping into my finances, marriage, social circle, and my artistic pursuits. Just about every area of my life has been plagued at one time or another by the nagging sensation I am not enough to experience genuine happiness.

WHERE IS THE LOVE?

When we are in a long-term committed relationship, it is common to feel disillusioned with our partner. The confines of marriage and child-rearing can easily become the place where passion goes to die. I had an acquaintance confide she left her husband because she arrived at a place where she could not stand him and she could no longer tolerate the person she was in his presence. This sort of contempt bred in familiarity grows insidiously throughout a couple's bonding. The years roll by while contentment is slowly chiseled away and replaced with complacency in the day-to-day business of life under our roofs. The pursuit and pressure of earning a living and supporting a family — with all of the challenges that come with it — throw women and men alike into roles that feel rigid and difficult. Personal fulfillment takes a back seat to obligations. We begin to ignore our desires and intuition. We become exhausted by the never-ending list of tasks that must be completed to keep the wheels in motion. We stop doing the little things that used to bring joy. When two people who see something attractive in each other come together and then gradually shut themselves off from the joys that used to light them up, it is easy to foresee the inevitable breakdown of their union.

A marriage or relationship becomes devoid of passion and intimate connection because *both* parties have allowed it to happen. Taking half the blame doesn't feel good, so we cast ourselves as the tragic hero and assign our partner the role of villain. Of course, one person may value work or parenting over being a spouse leaving their partner neglected. Perhaps substance abuse or infidelity is the issue. It is both parties' unwillingness to confront the issue(s) at hand that break apart the connection a couple requires to grow and thrive.

At some point, we make the unconscious decision that remaining unhappy is better than examining the reasons for its existence. We experience so much pain and anger over our relationships and lack of happy feelings they generate. We become overwhelmed by our emotions and cannot clearly articulate our feelings. Living with this kind of daily frustration, coupled with the building pressure of our self-imposed domestic culture, snuffs out our desire for our partner and for life in general.

We go numb as our coping mechanism. Our social media boasts an attractive wedding picture of a couple who has been together for twenty-five years and going strong but where would that union be without the support of Netflix, Betty Crocker, or Woodbridge Sauvignon Blanc? Numbing in the moment feels like an effective coping strategy because it provides us with temporary relief from our frustrations. The problem with numbing-out feelings of dissatisfaction is it numbs out feelings of happiness along with it. Numbing practices function as a general anesthetic on the human psyche. Bingeing on food, alcohol, television, online shopping, gaming; whatever brings escape. Over time it dulls our senses disconnecting us from our ability to feel joy and contentment of any kind.

HAVE SOME FREAKING FUN, ALREADY

Longevity alone is not proof of a happy marriage. In order for a marriage to truly thrive, a couple has to learn how to properly air disagreements, overcome hurt, embrace forgiveness, look for good in each other and consciously and consistently *make* the time to have fun together.

It wasn't a coincidence I noticed a huge improvement in my marriage the year my whole family took up alpine skiing. Every weekend we packed up a cooler of tasty snacks and headed up into the Gatineau Hills. The kids were dropped off to their ski instructors while my husband and I enjoyed a glorious ninety minutes to ourselves. We spent our time on the chairlift talking about long-forgotten dreams we wanted to accomplish — me to write a book, him to be self-employed. We talked freely about subjects we can't discuss around the children, laughed our heads off at all the inappropriate jokes we hadn't yet had the opportunity to share with each other and used cuss words liberally. We enjoyed the sensation of freely skiing down the hill without having to be preoccupied by anyone's safety other than our own. These precious ninety minutes together were so enjoyable my husband and I started making a few midweek ski dates together so we could continue connecting throughout the winter. I can tell you without reservation the money we've spent over the years on ski lessons, season passes, and equipment has been one of the best investments we've made in our marital health and costs far less than a divorce legal team.

WORK IS A FOUR-LETTER WORD

Those of us who combine family life with careers endure a double whammy of a beating from the expectation stick. Women in particular, who have to push against pay inequity, gender biases and setback careers after maternity leave, feel like they've jumped from the frying pan into the fire.

Over the course of two maternity leaves, I heard many women confide they ended up requiring pharmaceutical help to deal with their anxiety about returning to the workforce post-baby. No fussy baby ever settled itself at 2:00 a.m., to let its exhausted mother catch a few zzz's before giving her big presentation to the board of directors in the morning. Realizing your work is suffering and you are not performing at the same level as before baby is an unsettling feeling for most of us.

I can recall how fuzzy-headed I felt after months of sleep deprivation. I was desperately trying to choreograph competitive dance routines feeling like I was required to be creative at gunpoint. I couldn't think clearly, couldn't come up with clear artistic concepts or visions. I felt I had become a failure. It took everything I had to keep going. I pushed myself harder during this time than ever before yet felt I had very little to show for it. I just kept my head down, plowing through my difficulties, speaking to no one about how vulnerable and insecure I was about my ability to be a competent teacher. Each time something didn't turn out the way I had envisioned, I would silently berate myself for it and vow to work harder the next time.

Strategies such as these never yield good results. They invite depression, disillusionment, and career burnout. And that was exactly the place I found myself in the spring of 2011. I had arrived at a place where I felt completely drained by my career, totally uninspired, and unable to keep up. I needed a new plan.

BOUNDARIES
THEY'RE NOT JUST FOR CREEPY CO-WORKERS

One of the biggest pitfalls of being a teacher as well as an author is the lack of clearly defined work hours. This is particularly true of freelance contractors and all creative types who don't even leave their homes to earn their income. They get up, make coffee, flip on the computer and just like that, their workday has begun and extends into the evening hours. When the hours and physical environment of work and home meld together you find yourself feeling slightly fuzzy-headed and easily irritated with your family a great deal of the time. Logging in all hours, checking texts and emails while juggling all the facets of domestic life fractures and deteriorates your attention span. Look a squirrel!

Stress-response chemicals like cortisol and adrenaline pump through your veins. Few of us would ever encourage our adolescent children to post on social media while simultaneously completing household chores and working on important school projects, yet we justify a similar punishment on ourselves.

When I set myself the task of juggling motherhood and teaching dance with writing a book, I had to be strategic how I carved time out for each activity to have my undivided attention. I quickly learned that I should *never* try to write prose when the kids are home. I require complete solitude to transfer my ideas from thought to screen. Loading social media posts or website work could be done in their presence but always with a preannounced time constraint. Everyone knew when I was once again approachable for requests. "Mom, can I have a snack?"

I noticed how much better mornings were for the mental work of class planning or writing and how the afternoon was preferable for the physical work of house chores. Bit by bit, I learned how to create a schedule for myself that functioned for me instead of against me. Even on days when I only completed two tasks, I felt more productive than if I had started and abandoned twelve. I learned to stop at least thirty minutes before the first child arrived home from school to allow myself the time to reacclimatize to being outside of my own head. That was my time to blare Patty Smyth and mercilessly belt out the lyrics to *Warrior* as I moved around the house collecting laundry and dirty dishes.

Another crucial way to bring order to the chaos was by adopting business hours when I would respond to work texts and emails. I enforced a non-negotiable no-tech-at-the-table rule. Family dinner was to enjoy the food and company. It was a chance for everyone to flesh out the good, the bad, and the ugly of their day away from home.

BECOME A LIFELONG STUDENT

I once met a lady who confessed she envied my career in dance education. "It must be so nice to have this thing all for you that is completely outside the sphere of life at home." She, a stay-at-home-mom and former speech-language pathologist, greatly missed the stimulation of the outside world. I found myself completely sympathizing with her pain.

Here's a big truth-telling moment for me: I am so grateful I got to be at home during the day with my babies. We saved a pile in child-care expenses and my children spent their days with someone who loved them and was always up for a little adventure. But those years left me with an almost PTSD-like reaction of constantly humming "Old McDonald Had a Farm" to myself and swaying back and forth any time I found myself standing in a line for more than thirty seconds. I started losing interest in my vocation, as well as any form of media that wasn't related to parenting. Slowly it started to feel like my brain had turned into the same consistency of the homemade baby food I was making.

While I would not trade in those precious years with my babies, it would be grossly inaccurate for me to sit here and lead you to believe those years brought me joy and fulfillment. The truth is they were damn tough — physically and mentally. I felt just as starved for intellectual stimulation as I was for sleep. I was so lost in the rabbit hole of Diego and Baby Jaguar that I didn't think I'd ever surface. It was there I realized there were many things I could do to kick-start my brain again. It started with reading the newspaper and listening to talk radio. I started watching educational video clips with my husband on PBS Spacetime. I picked at free online courses and learned about physics, art history, world religions and did algebra for two months (btw … I still suck at math)!

I listened to motivational podcasts which led to dusting off my half-completed manuscript, hiring a writing coach, taking an online marketing course, and voilà! I once again entered the world of an adult who was fully engaged in passionate pursuits. I felt a renewed sense of purpose. I was interested in things and therefore became interesting. My proudest moment came when my husband and I were at a social function and I realized I had gone ninety whole minutes without talking about the kids!

After returning to my career as a dance teacher I found myself in a bit of a rut. Things were feeling stale and uninspired. I decided to use my time off in the summer to take courses and pursued a variety of dance classes, some geared to teaching, others to being a student and simply worked on my own technique. Some of these classes were outside my comfort zone and made me feel incredibly awkward but they all reconnected me with my passion for dance. When September rolled around, I was delighted to discover how excited I was to return to the classroom and instruct.

REKINDLE THE EMBERS OF PASSION

Living your life with passion has a wonderful butterfly effect into other areas of your life. Passionate people are enthusiastic and excited about their days. They find things to feel grateful for and use their gratitude as a conduit to create more joy for themselves. When you get involved in what lights you up and makes your heart sing, you are having more fun — and you're also more fun to be around! You feel alive —as in experiencing life — not just putting one foot in front of another and plowing through it.

You'll also have a better ability to handle your unique set of stressors. You use mental clarity and perspective to realize having a bad day doesn't mean you are having a bad life. Making the time to pursue your own passions makes you supportive of the people around you to do the same. If you're resentful of the time your spouse spends at the gym or all the time you spend driving your kids to activities, it could be a signal to make space for your own needs and desires within the family unit.

You are not a selfish shrew for insisting your yoga and pottery class go into the priority rotation. If your family isn't initially supportive of your need to reclaim me time then some gentle yet persistent retraining may be required. Remember, the whole reason they've come to rely on you for everything is because you've trained them to do so. We are mostly to blame for creating the needy demands of our mini-monsters; like it or not. Your family isn't doing anything to you that you aren't allowing. If you are unhappy here, it is up to you to gather your courage, grab the wheel and begin making a course correction. Like most expeditions into uncharted territory, it will be scary and unsettling. You will doubt what you are doing and where you are going. You may be tempted to throw in the towel and just keep going with the flow but then you'll miss the huge payoff.

Imagine what it would be like to sit around the dinner table with your family and have your own exciting discoveries and experiences to share. Remember what it was like when you and your husband were dating and had new topics to discuss? Remember that feeling when you were younger and you'd wake up excited to do something or go somewhere? Pursuing your own interests gives you back some of that energy. That's a mighty fine place to be and will have a huge impact on your marital satisfaction and your parenting.

There is an art and craft to domestic life that extends beyond what you do for family on a daily basis. We feel the most satisfaction in our personal lives when we learn how to combine the necessity for routine with the desperate need for novelty. Novelty is essential for artistic growth and is a major factor in personal contentment. As Gretchen Rubin says in her book, *The Happiness Project*, "Novelty, challenge and an atmosphere of growth are all necessary when attempting to cultivate happiness." So go to that foreign film, art museum or burlesque peepshow. Take that hip-hop class, learn archery, Italian or rally racing. The only thing more ridiculous than the thought of you doing any of those things is you hiding your desire to try any of them out! You have one life to live (unless of course, you're a Buddhist, in which case I will say that you will never be you again!)

This is your shot at being a happy, whole and fulfilled person. Right now. Today. So go forth and sign yourself up for those sky-diving lessons; just make sure to first update your life insurance and check off the organ donation section on your driver's license.

CHOOSE YOUR COMPANION PLANTS WISELY

The concept of companion planting in a garden

is a simple and effective way to ensure the seedlings you put into the ground will grow and thrive. Certain plants, when grouped together, provide ample support and strength for each other by increasing soil nutrients and repelling common pests. Take, for example, tomato and basil plants. Not only is basil a great supporting cast member in the grand production of pasta sauce, it also lends a hand in the garden as well! This herb works overtime to help the tomato plant produce a higher yield of crops while inoculating it from the ravages of mosquitoes and flies. The tomato plant grows beautifully alongside basil. With support like that, how could it not?

Other plants such as potatoes tend to have the opposite effect. Tomatoes and potatoes are susceptible to the same mildew fungus that produces rot. Planting them too close together results in the creation of a superhighway for spreading disease.

Sometimes we set our roots down in an unfavorable plot. We plant ourselves next to people who do not support us and instead spread their own brand of rot. This can be a tricky area to navigate when we are put into situations where we don't get to choose the people in our environment; work, the parent associations at our children's schools, or even those with whom we share our DNA.

I've met many miserable souls in the various places I've worked and volunteered over the years. These people were all dealing with exceptionally difficult or painful circumstances in at least one area of their personal lives. As a result, they developed a cynical attitude toward their spouses, their work, their children's teachers and life in general. Many of them would use the people around them as dumping sites for toxic emotions they didn't know how to release. These energy suckers are quick to criticize yet remain highly sensitive to receiving criticism. They cultivate an attitude of intolerance for the shortcomings of others and rarely have a kind word for anyone who is not present in the room. When you spend time with people who operate from this negative mindset, you are severely crippling your own ability to grow, thrive and experience feelings of well-being.

With their brooding misery and surly dispositions, miserable people will drain all the nutrients from those around them and leave you feeling as if you are covered with a powdery fungus. You feel drained, zoned-out, ashamed or uncomfortable in the presence of your garden-mates. Their company is exhausting. You rarely get a word in edgewise. You often fear your opinions will be judged. Here's a simple way to tell if you are rooted next to a toxic plant. If you walk away from an engagement where you spent time with someone and you left feeling *joyful*, you've got yourself a tomato-basil arrangement. If you walk away from your time together feeling *joyless*, you've got a tomato-potato deal.

Joyless can also feel like insecurity or confusion. Either way, you toss the salad, you've attached yourself to someone who gathers their energy by tearing others down instead of building them up. It is wise to spend as little time as possible with people of this nature. Be busy when they call you. When you have to deal with them at work or other mutual organizations, raise the shields to maximum capacity. Don't engage in their gossip. Change the subject when they want to complain about the people who aren't in the room. Remain positive, polite, and detached. Soon their tendrils will dry up and they will no longer be reaching for you. Walk away. You haven't lost a darn thing.

I've learned many valuable lessons from my plants in the years I've spent playing in the dirt. Just like the Diablo Ninebark I've come to realize resiliency plays an integral part in the progression toward a happy life. If you can stop waiting for things to work out in your favor before you feel happy and choose to begin each day with a joyful mindset; living a contented existence becomes a lot simpler. Whether the soil around you is dry, evenly moist, or hard-packed, you have the ability to expand and strengthen your root system and bloom no matter where you are planted.

ADHERE TO PERSEVERE

THINK LIKE A COYOTE

"Success is not final, failure is not fatal: it is the courage to continue that counts."
—Winston Churchill

My all-time favorite Bugs Bunny episode from childhood is the one where Wile E. Coyote (super genius) has just received his Acme bat suit and is trying it out for the first time. This is the latest scheme in his repertoire of half-baked plots to catch the elusive Road Runner.

As a child of the eighties, I had seen this episode more times than I could possibly count. Still I find myself cracking up at the sight of the super genius, covered head to toe in green rubber, opening his impressive wingspan and jumping off a rocky cliff. Although he looks completely ridiculous, the self-confidence he exudes at his ability to maneuver the rocky terrain below and air currents above is nothing short of impressive.

No matter how many times I see it, I just can't get over the smug look on his face mid-flight. He's so sure of himself even though he's flying for the first time in his life. The entertainment value in watching him smack into the rock-face that appears out of nowhere borders on uncontrollable hilarity. It will never get old.

But part of me sympathizes to the point of agony with my doomed canine counterpart. I have felt the same way he does every time his best-laid plan goes up in smoke.

We've all had crummy days. As I write this, I am coming off the granddaddy of all crummy days. Today began with me feeling I had this grown-up thing down pat and was actually the real deal for once instead of a cheap imitation.

Did you happen to catch that green blur in the sky yesterday afternoon?

Yup, that was me wearing my own Acme bat suit.

While you were toiling away at your daily tasks, I was soaring into the atmosphere mastering the art of "adulting." Not only was I managing my adult responsibilities, but I was *enjoying* them. One nanosecond after I glanced around to make certain your eyes were admiring how well put-together I've become — BANG! I flattened myself against the side of a boulder.

We all encounter boulders in our paths from time to time. Mine take the form of rejection letters from magazines, an overdrawn checking account, unanticipated automobile repairs, flooding basements, a forgotten appointment, unfavorable parent-teacher interviews … the list is endless.

I am tempted to give in to the strong impulse to curl up in the fetal position and scratch the silk borders off all of my daughter's baby blankets. I want to hang a "Closed for Business" sign around my neck and tell everyone who depends on me to take a hike.

Something has gone awry at the Acme distribution warehouse. If they knew my order of patience, maturity and competence has been discontinued they would quit showing up to ask things of me.

Then I ask myself … what would Wile E. Coyote do?

Would he pack it in, become a vegetarian and start a soy and lima bean farm?

No. I think not.

After he peeled himself off the side of his latest boulder, he would dust himself off and go back to the drawing board. Although most of his ideas are a little to the left of successful, you have to admire his perseverance. He's not one for wallowing in self-pity, that Mr. Coyote.

He's a mover.

He's a shaker.

He makes things happen.

When they don't work out, he makes something else happen.

Damn, I want to be a coyote when I grow-up.

Being a successful adult does not mean my life is running as smoothly as an over-rehearsed theatrical script.

It means when those boulders make their appearances, I will give myself time to appraise my situation, learn my lesson and repair. I may have to slow down, but afterward, I'll keep going.

There will be days when all I do is pick sand and small pebbles out of my teeth (really can't say enough about the importance of closed-mouth aviation), but after I've had some time to lick my wounds I'll be on the phone with Acme's first available representative to order the next highly acclaimed invention.

One day that Road Runner will be mine.

FAILURE: MAKE IT EPIC!

Many of life's failures are people who did not realize how close they were to success when they gave up."
—Thomas Edison

Success is a subjective and inflammatory goal. When I first started writing seriously I defined success as a complete novel manuscript. After completing my manuscript I was still unsatisfied. How amazing would it be if I could get my novel published! If I could become a published author I would feel legitimately successful. Soon I received an offer to publish. I was thrilled. But it wasn't long before I started dreaming about the next level of authorial success. The words *bestseller* began taunting me. *Sure*, I told myself, *getting published is great, but truly successful authors are ones who actually make an income from their writing and get to see their names on important recognizable lists.*

Little by little, my definition of success relied more and more on outside validation. Each time I climbed another rung on the ladder, I'd hold my breath and wonder, *Will it be good enough?*

Creating art from an authentic place requires a certain amount of sacrifice on the part of the artist. The biggest sacrifice an artist must make is to relinquish her desire to know if people will "get" or like her work. She must shift her priority from *belonging* to *being*.

When an artist has the ability to create and share her work without fearing how others will perceive it, she is free to grow an idea to fruition. Every artist is primarily motivated by an idea not seen by the rest of the world. Sharing these parts of ourselves should not be the gateway to discouragement. Your self-worth should never be based on the approval of others. Public opinion is subjective. Measuring your value on a fickle sliding scale will leave you feeling empty and worthless.

Sadly, this is not the way our society functions. Many of us, artists and non-artists alike, experience crippling personal crises. Meltdowns take root disconnecting us from our God-given talents. Believing the images that are reflected back, we accept our lack of value. We are not enough. We begin to define ourselves by our lack of universal praise.

This affliction is not only limited to the artist. We all want that pat on the back. All of us are hungry to be seen by others and recognized for our worth. We look for this validation in our careers, appearance, home décor, involvement in volunteering and killer recipe for peach pie. We gladly exhaust ourselves all in the name of acceptance. When will it be enough? When will we learn to give this to ourselves?

Paradoxically, achieving great success also presents similar pitfalls. Now we have set a precedent. What if future endeavors fail to live up to the defined level of expectation? What does that say about us and our inability to fill our own shoes? Here lies the problem of projecting ourselves into the horrors of an imagined future. The only way out of this suffering is to shut-off the anxiety valve and reset our brains. Artists who practice meditation to quiet their racing minds are much better at avoiding this pitfall as they have consciously trained themselves to be present. The key is to remember creation happens in the heart, not the head. So stay out of yours. You will never find your muse hanging out with fear and self-loathing.

Success requires surrendering to failure. When we refuse to sit with failure, we decline the opportunity for growth. Every failure is a lesson bringing you closer to your goal. We all begin somewhere. There's no shame in having your climb begin at rock bottom.

Soon after my young adult novel, *True Colours*, was published, I received notice the company who published my novel was being sold. All titles would be transferred to another publishing house. When I submitted my sequel novel publication, I endured a lengthy and agonizing wait with no response. After nearly a year of waiting, I received an official rejection. I could have kept trying but I was busy telling myself the laundry list of reasons why writing professionally would never work out for me. Lack of expertise, time, money, needing to prioritize my family blah, blah, blah. Returning to negative self-talk I permitted myself to let go of the very thing that feeds my spirit the most. Eventually, I learned my failure to get the sequel published wasn't so much due to a lack of resources as it was to a lack of my own resourcefulness. Instead of seeing my situation as an opportunity to explore other tools at my disposal, I chose to take the rejection personally and viewed it as proof I wasn't talented enough. I didn't ask for critical feedback. I didn't utilize platforms like writers' groups to see how other authors overcame these stumbling blocks. I didn't investigate the avenue of self-publishing. What I did do was channel my angst into Cabernet Sauvignon and Netflix — two of my besties who rarely let me down. In short, I gave up. End of story.

This time I chose to write myself a new story. This time, I chose to MAKE and KEEP the time to write every day. I chose to dust off that long-forgotten manuscript where I had recorded my personal insights I dreamed of sharing with other women. I took an online self-publishing course. I joined writers' groups and started networking. I listened to their ideas for improvement. I consciously worked every day to move myself toward my dreams. I used positive visualization as a tool to keep up my energy levels and motivation. If you are not my family and are reading this book right now, you have just proven the effectiveness of this approach.

As for that nagging little voice that keeps telling me I have no business here … she is currently enjoying an imaginary all-expenses-paid trip to the Canary Islands. I figured her sour disposition was a telltale sign she was in need of a vacation. I truly hope she is enjoying herself.

Facing failure means accepting your current method isn't working and you're open to explore other ways. This is how we learn. This is how we grow. This is how we succeed.

Living with an open heart and not referring to the script of the stories we tell ourselves is our life raft from the sinking ship of self-destruction. When we see failure as a temporary pit stop on the road to success, we have the opportunity to use our setbacks as a catapult toward our goals.

Perhaps you are in a similar place in your life. You are searching for the best version of yourself as an artist, scientist, athlete, entrepreneur, teacher or parent. Remember … the difference between failure ending your journey or be a turning point is your perspective. This will determine whether it will have *power over you* or be

something that *empowers you*.
> The destination awaits you.
> The journey is what makes you.

FOR BETTER OR WORSE
AN ANTHOLOGY OF MARRIAGE

"A successful marriage requires falling in love many times, always with the same person." —Mingon McLaughlin

The institution of marriage, like the bustier you wore under your wedding dress, is as old as dirt. Despite its ceremonial longevity, marriage has evolved considerably over the centuries. Where it once revolved around securing land, wealth and titles, it now serves as the ultimate expression of couple bonding in Western civilization. While the feminist in me is thrilled about the idea of living in a society that has evolved beyond arranged marriages, I feel this set the stage a long time ago for us to get many things wrong in marriage. As a lifetime learner who has done an extensive residency in marriage over the last two decades, I would like to share with you my experiences in the three marriages I have experienced to date.

MYTH #1: MARRIAGE WILL BRING YOU HAPPINESS

On the morning of my wedding day, I rose early, slapped on a pair of rollerblades, and went for a five-kilometer jaunt beside the picturesque Ottawa River Parkway. I passed a robe-clad monk-ish looking fellow who lived nearby and frequently strolled the same path. I remember as I approached him from behind, he stopped and turned toward me. I must have crossed paths with this gentleman at least a dozen times or more that summer. He never once acknowledged me. But on this particular morning, he beamed a genuine smile at me and spoke the words that I will never forget: *"Your joy is beautiful."*

Those words certainly reflected what I was feeling inside. The elation and excitement of my wedding day was a unique euphoria that never repeated again during the course of that first marriage. It was a truly beautiful day from start to finish. In my naivety, I believed I had found my happy ending, joined with the person who would love me forever, whom I would love forever and we would experience the kind of happiness I had been longing for throughout my twenties. Imagine my surprise when four years later, after acquiring the usual accoutrements of a house and a baby, I found myself completely miserable. Neither my husband nor I felt anything remotely close to happiness. On the rare occasions when we would go out to dinner alone, I would look with envy upon the couples who were smiling and speaking softly to each other. They took enjoyment from each other's company. We were both angry, exhausted and blamed the other for the canyon of resentment growing between us. What my then-husband and I had failed to realize was marriage is not an end goal that would make us happy. Marriage, contrary to popular belief, has very little to offer in the way of happiness. What it can promise you is a bit of paperwork (both at the onset and during tax season), half of your mattress real estate, two sets of dirty dishes in the sink and shared custody of the television's remote control.

Love, attention, support, laughter, enjoyment … those are feelings found in people who consistently and consciously infuse those desired emotions into their marriages each and every day. When both partners do their share, the marriage is a positive, grounding force in the couple's lives. When the partners overdraw their joint marriage account but rarely make any deposits, disappointment, resentment, and disengagement take root and spread. It taints the way we see our partners. This is when we start feeling as if we have made a mistake, chosen unwisely, have "fallen out of love," or simply just "can't do it anymore."

When we think back to our courting days with our present long-term partner, we recall how easily and naturally it was to be together. We felt lit-up in their presence, could easily talk together, sharing for hours. We were so focused on the feelings we were receiving from our new relationship we barely noticed our own actions.

We don't remember how we used to greet our partners with a smile and an embrace rather than a grunt or a complaint about a lousy day. We don't recall how we used to call each other on the phone just to connect and hear each other's voices rather than to lament the expense of automobile repairs. We don't remember a time when our priority was to offer our assistance rather than demand an expectation be met. In other words, we don't remember the days of treating the other person with the same level of courtesy, engagement, attention, and uplifting energy we typically offer to other acquaintances.

We go about our day giving our best to employers, coworkers, students, clients, heck, even complete strangers, only to go home and give what's left of ourselves to our spouses. We begin tangoing with thoughts that whisper *"unfulfilled," "waiting to die," "I deserve to be happy,"* while oblivious to the fact we have actively participated in creating our current misery. Happiness in marriage is directly proportionate to the healthy and energetic currency being deposited by both parties into their joint account. This is what my husband and I just did not understand. The marriage ended.

MYTH #2 MARRIAGE SHOULD BE EQUAL

After a proper amount of time spent on

introspection and wound licking, I decided to jump back into the fire and take another crack at this whole marriage thing. One thing that marriage number two had going for it was a better sense of sharing the household responsibilities. I remember early on in that second union, marveling at how the new guy would do dishes without being asked or regarding it as some huge favor. I was so taken with this guy's attitude and felt so supported I happily added another child to our family unit. To my delight, hubby number two kept doing the dishes, laundry and even started cooking dinner on some nights. I started thinking all of our domestic dealings should be equally divided. I mean, fair is fair, right? Gradually, over time, my new partner-in-crime began dropping the ball. Some things started to get pushed onto the back burner. Some things weren't even done at all. I was so stuck on equality I shut out the opportunity for each of us to shine where we genuinely had something valuable to offer.

Life is rarely even and fair and marriage echoes this sentiment. You may do all of the cooking. He may do all of the yard work. You are the go-to liaison for parent-teacher interviews. He handles all the insurance renewals. The main consideration in your division of household responsibilities is you are each contributing to the functionality of family life. Complete symmetry clashes with practical application. Domestic harmony demands consistent communication. "Sweetheart, I'm going to be slammed with report cards all day and won't be able to cook dinner this evening. Can I leave this in your wheelhouse tonight? I'm fine with whatever you pick up on your way in."

Flexible branches are resilient in storms.
Rigid branches are not.

MYTH # 3 CONFLICT IN MARRIAGE IS BAD

After many back-and-forth battles over household responsibilities, I found myself completely drained. A relationship should not feel so difficult so much of the time. I mean, the right partnership should sustain you, not drain you, correct? My new husband and I were good at connecting with each other on a personal level. I was receiving more consideration than I had ever known in my first marriage, yet I shied away from any issue of conflict. My husband, who was also exhausted by these rows, also shifted into ostrich mode and stuck his head into the biggest sand dune he could find. As a result of our unwillingness to deal with conflict and the uncomfortable ensuing emotions that marriage also ended.

Once again, it was time to cue up R.E.M.'s "Everybody Hurts," crack open and devour an entire bag of Old Dutch BBQ chips, and turn to the support of my trusted associates Gin & Tonic. Upon assessing my second marriage, I realized the drive-you-out-of-your-mind irritation, the I-hate-myself-when-I'm-around-you-and-want-to-stab-you-in-the-ear-with-a-paté-spreader has nothing to do with the issue at hand and everything to do with all that has been left unsaid between you and your partner. We are so uncomfortable with confrontation we cannot bring ourselves to have those big discussions. We sweep the dirt under the rug until it reaches the ceiling and pushes us face-first into the wall.

What hubby number two and I didn't realize was perpetual conflict is not necessarily a sign you should go your separate ways. Conflict is a calling to roll up your sleeves and peel back another layer in your relationship's evolution. Avoiding the bitter flavor of conflict denies you the chance to experience real growth together. Being open to conflict develops a new maturity, respect, compassion, and love in your relationship. A rewarding adult relationship isn't the result of good fortune or meeting the "right" person. It's the result of two hard-working people who prioritize fleshing out their weaknesses and building up each other's strengths.

MYTH #4 MARRIAGE SHOULD BE YOUR IDENTITY

So I embraced my headstrong (ahem, stubborn) nature and found things to admire about my new beau's headstrong (ahem, stubborn) nature as well. I worked hard on making my big, scary, passionate emotions work for me and finally I was mature enough to enter a healthy relationship. The new man felt the same way about his previous experiences and we mutually decided we would be great marriage partners.

For a time, things were great. Both husband number three and I were consciously using the tools we had acquired in our previous relationships to have more satisfying exchanges. I became completely immersed in marriage and motherhood. I worked hard at identifying my feelings, being available for my new husband and the kids, taking pride in maintaining our lives and home.

Slowly but surely, I parted with things from the outside world, telling myself I was too busy to enjoy them. Things like writing, taking dance classes (as in classes not taught by me), reading lengthy novels, taking long, lingering walks and the guilty pleasure of watching movies that have no interest for anyone besides myself. Why? Because I had to bake muffins for the kids' lunches, and I had to make certain that my husband's shirts were cleaned. The toilets needed to be scrubbed. I had already worked three evenings this week and needed to be home to tuck the kids in. Meet you for lunch on Wednesday? Sorry, no can do. I'm helping to make four hundred hotdogs at the kids' school. What do you mean that's crazy? Good parents pitch in and have a strong presence at their children's school. Everybody knows that!

I had many reasons why the flow of life inside

the home was more important than maintaining space for myself. I didn't pursue things outside of the home that added value to my own, individual life. I lost myself. You'll never believe this next part, but guess what? I started feeling deeply unhappy. My entire life's purpose was to serve and support my family. I did that job so well I started resenting them for it. Now if you can follow the trail of breadcrumbs leading from my need to be Supermom to my spectacular collapse, you will recognize the pervasive need to always be caring for others while neglecting yourself has nothing to do with them and everything to do with you.

Some of us turn to substance abuse to cope with our feelings of unhappiness. Some have affairs. A boatload of us use frantic, thoughtless overwork (paid or unpaid) as a means of escape. Operating from a "the more I do, the more I am" principle, the workaholic seeks validation through the achievement of tasks. Carving out an exterior identity of competence is more favorable than the inner one of worthlessness. While people who operate this way seem super organized and reliable, ultimately they are unhappy, unbalanced individuals who have great difficulty maintaining contentment in their close personal relationships.

MYTH #5 MARRIAGE SHOULD BE EMOTIONALLY SYMBIOTIC

Let's all geek out and talk science for a moment, shall

we? There's this interesting theory in quantum physics known as quantum entanglement. Quantum entanglement suggests groups or pairs of particles that interact, or share a spatial proximity have the ability to affect each other's quantum state. Particles are now unable to act independently of the other even when they are separated by large distances. Make sense? Yeah, me neither.

Let's try again:

Let's pretend that two electrons (we'll call them Particle A and Particle B) collide by a chance meeting in space, spend some time together and then go their separate ways. Now separated by a vast amount of space, we see that what happens to one particle mysteriously affects the other. This phenomenon was labeled as "spooky action from a distance" by a scientific dude with an enviable head of hair. Who knew that Albert Einstein's findings in the realm of quantum physics would also have such relevance in the psychology of marriage?

Now let's call Particle A John and Particle B Jane. John and Jane meet at a party. After a few drinks and chit-chat, they decide that they dig each other, start spending time together, divulge intimate knowledge of each other's lives, go to Mexico together, shack up, buy furniture, get a dog, buy a condo, have a beautiful ceremony in Maui and become life partners. Fast forward five years later.

John and Jane have intertwined their lives to the point that Jane has become keenly sensitive to John's unhappiness at work. John returns from work miserable on most nights. He is listless and irritable. He feels trapped in a job he hates but is required to help maintain their standard of living. He's slipping into some kind of career-related depression. Jane is most upset by this shift in John's emotional state. She is so empathetic to John's misery that she cooks all his favorite meals, plans special outings and spends a great deal of her energy trying to make him feel happy again. No matter her effort, she can't seem to snap him out of it. She wants things to go back to the happy-go-lucky days of their early courtship and feels extremely frustrated with the emotional current in their home. Jane is starting to feel depressed herself even when John is not around. She begins to confide in her female friends. They confirm her worst suspicions: John is a major downer. His melancholy is ruining their lives. It is his fault that Jane is unhappy.

Emotional entanglement results in a great deal of misery for everyone involved. In fact, this was the straw that broke the camel's back in my third marriage. After examining my declining emotional state and working to reconnect with who was still inside of me that did not answer to the names Mom or Mrs, hubby number three informed me that he could no longer cope with a depressed wife. Here was a guy who also had been around the block with more than one marriage under his belt. He'd done a pile of work on himself yet could not make his current wife happy. He took my unhappiness in our marriage as a sign of a lack of love. Ours was not an acceptable living arrangement for him. That summer, though we continued to live under the same roof, my husband and I spent a great deal of time apart. We worked at unpacking our emotional baggage, teased out what belonged to whom, and severed our entangled emotional connection. One night, over two steaming cups of tea, we talked quietly with our heads bent and thanked the other for the support which allowed our growth throughout the relationship. We realized a grave error. We unfairly made our own happiness contingent upon the other's happiness. We decided that it was best to end our marriage.

In healthy partnerships, we are able to provide emotional support for our partners without absorbing their feelings and making them our own. When our partners are going through difficulty, we are able to be there for them, make space for their troubled emotions and allow them to lean on us. But we remain detached enough to still feel our individual emotional climate. We don't make ourselves responsible for their well-being. We keep our potential to experience happiness even if our partners are experiencing sorrow, despair, or anger. If your partner is experiencing a headache and you have an overwhelming need to take an Advil, something's definitely out of whack.

Entanglement becomes our unhealthy normal. While we hate to admit it, most of us feel defined by our marriage's shortcomings. We endure the quiet shame of failure.

I end my own marriage anthology by letting you know the morning after I ended marriage number three, I sat across the breakfast table from the man who would become husband number four. Despite what you may think, I was not racking up frequent flyer miles with an online dating account. Each time I began a new marriage I began it with the same man. This is difficult, but not impossible. Many of you are doing this right now. Without realizing it, you are in the trenches recording the history of your own marriage anthologies, forging your own endings and new beginnings. Maybe your story includes a dark and painful chapter known as divorce, where you learned to face your fears, claim a newfound resiliency and navigate the waters of co-parenting with a former partner. Whether you stay or leave for good, both paths lead to greater understanding of yourself and how you relate to the most significant people in your life. This is the greatest gift offered to those who are ready to accept it.

Today's marriages come with something far more valuable than a dowry and a fatted calf. Today's marriages offer choices. With choice comes power: the power to choose how you will respond to the challenges that every marriage will inevitably face. In the end, whether we remain together, or we separate, it is not our problems that define us, but rather how we choose to respond to them.

    Our true character is discovered — for better or worse.

EUCLID'S ELEMENTS OF INTERPLANETARY MARRIAGE

"And the whole is greater than the part."
—*Euclid*

My husband and I originate from two different countries. This accounts for many of our differences. But sometimes I feel as though there is an entire solar system dividing our places of origin instead of an ocean. We aren't even on the same planet.

I come from a place where magic is created. I can watch a dance performance and be moved to tears. I hear a piece of music and feel goosebumps on my arms. I am tickled to laughter simply by using my ability to see the absurd in the most ordinary of moments. Sometimes, and this is by far my most preferred way to be inconvenienced, I feel the presence of a muse on my shoulder. She whispers in my ear as she caresses me with inspiration to write. This is all terribly distracting. I end up abandoning whatever task I was involved in to sit and shape my thoughts before she decides to fade into the ether and turn her favor to someone else who is open to her energy. All of these things are available to me because I come from the planet Artist.

It is easy to spot my kind. We can frequently be found picking ourselves up and brushing away the dirt from our clothes. Artists are notorious for tripping over roots and rocks because our focus is almost always directed skyward. Always reaching on the tips of our toes, trying to grasp that little gem of an idea by the tail and pull it into fruition. For an artist, there is no grander preoccupation than holding the potential of creative energy. We feel its weight in our palms and begin the process of massaging it from a cerebral concept into a tangible creation.

It's delicious.

It's consuming.

It's exhausting.

My husband, by contrast, hails from a place where the inhabitants are preoccupied with mathematical equations. Instead of fiction on his bedside table, you will find titles such as *CALCULUS: FOUNDATIONS AND APPLICATIONS, DATA STRUCTURES & DIGITAL COMPRESSION, CONCRETE MATHEMATICS, FINITE MATHEMATICS, PATTERN-ORIENTED SOFTWARE ARCHITECTURE,* and, of course, the riveting second edition of *FOUNDATIONS OF ALGORITHMS: EVERYTHING YOU WANTED TO KNOW BUT WERE AFRAID TO ASK.*

You see, my husband's place of origin is the

planet Geek.

People from planet Geek also pick themselves out of the dirt, but instead of gazing to the heavens above, their clumsiness is generally attributed to having their nose stuck in a book or screen. Many of these souls shine so brightly with intellectual genius they appear at times to lack basic social and interpersonal skills.

My husband is passionate about math. In fact, he refers to it as an art. It is, without a doubt, his preferred form of expression. It functions beautifully for him when constructing elegant software code, compressing data, generating digital images, all the myriad computer programming tasks I won't pretend to have a clue about.

Sadly, it does little to help him communicate with his family; his wife in particular. She has zero understanding of numbers and due to her choices in career is rarely required to count past eight. This chick's all about words, her husband's kryptonite.

What's a guy with a pocket full of algorithms to do?

My husband can be a sparkling conversationalist, particularly when it pertains to something he's keyed up about. Lately, his preferred interest lies in a book he's reading titled *Euclid's Elements*.

Euclid was a Greek mathematician often referred to as the "father of geometry." His system of geometry was hailed for its use of logic and demand of proof. He influenced many notable leaders, teachers, and philosophers, including Descartes, Newton, and Abraham

Lincoln. While every picture of this dude that I've ever seen has him dressed like a garden gnome (seriously, Google him), his body of work is unparalleled in the archives of the scientific/math community and has been referred to as the most influential nonreligious book of all time.

Way to go, Euclid!

One night, I returned home from the studio to find my husband eager to share something with me. He was excited about Euclid's proposition to construct an equilateral triangle out of one line segment by using circles. Basically, you can show the existence of a perfect triangle at the point where two circles intersect. This is not life-altering news. But for someone like my husband, Euclid's teachings offer a powerful muse in the ways of abstract logic.

"Do you see it?" my husband asks me excitedly. "Isn't that cool?"

I peer down at his drawing and assure him that the little triangle between the two circles is indeed cause for celebration. I raise my eyebrows and say things like "Wow!" and "Neato!"

Then I proceed to ask him if he's eaten today and how much sleep he's had in the last week.

This somehow spirals into a conversation about how math is the abstract expression of ideas. According to my husband, "ten" is only a way to express quantification and isn't really a number at all.

For a fleeting second, I wonder if he's on to something here. I proceed to ask him if he thinks we could convince the bank we don't actually owe them that really big number on the mortgage due to the fact that it doesn't actually exist. He doesn't think it's a good idea.

But I digress…

Numeric codification is an expression of an idea, much the same way that words are, or dance, or music … you see where this is going, right? My husband — my math-loving, code-generating, algorithm-obsessed husband — has just given me proof of his own brand of abstract logic.

It would appear my Euclidian pupil feels we are not so different. In fact, to quote one of Euclid's common notions: *Things that coincide with each other are equal to each other.* It is my husband's opinion that our likeness can be found in the place where our differences collide. In other words, he's constructed a mathematical equation to explain our relationship. Geek.

A statement of this nature requires proof, of course, so like any good student of logic, I show him my work.

Herein lies the overlapping of two circles: one right-brain-dominant, the other left. The merging of art, math, perceptual and conceptual thinking, creates its own little triangle: the union of words and numbers. Each is struggling to express its own abstract logic to its foreign counterpart.

It may not be perfect, but the very least, it's

educational and entertaining, that is until someone needs to find a set of car keys. My husband and I bring something completely different to the table (or should I say triangle?). He has shown me the value of using logic over feelings in certain situations. He has shown me that sometimes less is more and that silence can be powerful. He is also the reason that I have learned to follow a budget.

For my part, I think I've shown him the necessity for clear spoken communication with an emphasis on tone. I've shown him how feelings can sometimes be more important than logic and absolutely need to be voiced. I also believe it is acceptable to take credit for his ability to clean the kitchen properly and employ different character voices when reading stories to our children.

Lots of things are going on in that little triangle.

And so, to conclude this little geometry lesson on marital compatibility, I'm kind of happy my husband and I had our chance collision. I had my head in the clouds, courted by an idea, while he had his nose in a book, working out a mathematical equation. Two circles containing two opposite life forms, yet both governed by abstract, expressive thinking.

Perhaps the best thing to result from this little meeting of the minds is the appreciation we've both adopted for the other person's thought process and the way it has forced us to keep working on our relationship.

Always trying to solve problems from a different angle.

In other words, we keep calm and triangle on.

ODE TO ENVY

THE CULTURE OF COMPARISON

"Envy is the art of counting the other fellow's blessings
instead of your own."
—Harold Coffin

I have this friend. Let's call her Yvonne. Yvonne is a busy lady who juggles a full-time career and four children complete with various activities. She has a happy marriage and a lovely home. If that isn't enough to deepen the crease between your eyebrows, she also has a thriving social life full of people who love her. She's fulfilled by activities that deeply engage her.

Perhaps you too know Yvonne? The Yvonnes of the world shine brilliantly, no matter the weather forecast. They have great marriages and raise good kids. They use proper manners. They experience "job satisfaction." They follow through on things. I also suspect they floss with regularity and recycle.

Those Yvonnes have their shit together in a big way.

On some days, scrolling through Yvonne's shiny status updates and social media pictures makes me feel as if I have taken a wrong turn in the game of life. The nagging voices of discontent heckle me from a balcony tucked in the faraway corner of my brain. I feel that familiar, cavernous sense of emptiness start to expand in my chest. I start to wonder why I haven't yet found happiness. What have I done wrong?

What do I need to acquire to finally make me feel I have enough? How do I sit comfortably in my own skin, imperfections and all? Most importantly, how the hell do I become like Yvonne's Facebook?

Sadly, these questions rarely lead to answers. True happiness is just as elusive to define as it is to experience. But for the purpose of this essay, I suppose I should take a stab at it.

Happiness is not so much a state of having as a state of being. We must consciously choose to be happy each and every day if we want to feel at peace. That means we must actively train ourselves to tune into the frequency of feeling good about our lives. We create the reality of our lives through our thoughts. If we are in the habit of logging on to our social media pages, scrolling through brilliantly filtered images and cultivating feelings of envy, inadequacy, and boredom, that is exactly what we will experience. If we, the adult heads of our households, don't grasp this concept how on earth will our children fare? An overabundance of social media consumption can negatively impact young, developing minds. Experts are frequently warning parents against the dangers of allowing their adolescents to run amok on social media sites. All concerns for personal safety aside, social media holds the same pitfalls for adolescents as it does for many of us adults who are not rooted strongly enough in our own power. Social media is a wonderful way to publicize, advertise and stay connected to people we wouldn't regularly see. But it has another, darker side. The less self-assured among us have turned it into a marvelous tool for self-loathing and devaluation. We compare our lives with those beautifully poised and immaculately filtered digital images we consume.

Most adults are primarily concerned with teaching ethical internet use to their children. It is equally important to teach digital awareness. Be aware of your posting habits. Posting multiple selfies and comments then spending every spare moment of the day checking how people are reacting to them is just not healthy behavior. Social media culture has conditioned us to feel a sense of lack rather than gratitude. The problem here is not so much with social media sites themselves but rather how we use them for a quick fix of approval and validation. Without a strong sense of self, we focus our energy on gaining likes, followers, and subscribers. We base our self-worth on the feedback we receive from our online audience rather than learning how to give this to ourselves. When we are not fully engaged in our lives nor present in our own reality, we prefer to be immersed in an online universe. We catch ourselves habitually logging on, seeking the stimulation we desperately crave. Pop-up notifications ensure that we never stray too far. This allows us to keep one foot in the digital world at all times. It also keeps us in the stream of lower frequency emotions.

We are focused on what others have.

We are focused on what we don't have.

We are focused on trying to get people to pay attention to us.

We feel empty because we give our power away.

The people who experience the most contentment are those who work the hardest at cultivating an attitude of gratitude for the things that are *already in their lives.*

When you take the time to stop and pay attention to what's right in front of your face, you will realize that being happy isn't so unattainable after all. You can learn to appreciate the beautiful forest you're standing in — one tree at a time.

You become your own Yvonne.

Now, that I like.

THE ALCHEMY OF ROMANTIC LOVE

"It is our imagination hat is responsible for love, not the other person." —Marcel Proust

This morning I am walking the trails of my favorite conservation area. During my morning stroll, I encounter other people walking the path by the river, enjoying the lovely scenery. There is a quiet, muttered greeting exchanged between us as we pass. This happens with everyone I encounter with one exception – a couple who pass me, hand in hand, whispering and laughing quietly to themselves. We do not make eye contact as they draw near. My existence completely escapes their notice as we brush shoulders. So engulfed in their conversation nothing around interests them except the other person. I walk by with a building sense of irritation. Later in the day I am finally able to put my finger on what irks me so much about this particular couple. My ire has nothing to do with them and everything to do with me. With a mounting sense of humility, I realize I am jealous. This affectionate pair has stirred up an enviable longing for feelings I have not experienced in quite some time.

I have many wonderful things going for me in my life. My husband and I have a stable, committed marriage complete with a bustling and busy family life. We are surrounded by people we love. We pursue activities that bring delight.

But here's a nasty little truth-bomb: few pleasures in life can rival the magnitude of the amphetamine-like high you get from a new relationship. Long term committed relationships with all of their stability and comfort –things we longed for tremendously in our single days –have little to offer in this respect.

Ka-boom.

During the early stages of attraction, we think the object of our affection gives us that weightless feeling of happiness. Thanks to the research of notable anthropologist, Dr. Helen Fisher, author of *The Brain On Love*, we know the more accurate explanation is the brain chemical b-Phenylethylamine (PEA), a.k.a. "the love drug." PEA is responsible for the addictive jolt we experience with a new attraction. This brain chemical is produced by the pharmaceutical dispensing prankster in our skulls (we'll call him "Julio" just for fun) and lasts two years or so of a new relationship.

You Are Here

Lucy Lemay Cellucci

Julio is pouring out a powerful cocktail when you find yourself attracted to somebody new. One key ingredient is dopamine, a neurotransmitter that causes a sensation akin to a substance-induced high. According to the research of Dr. John Marsden, head of the British National Addiction Centre, dopamine is not unlike the rush experienced with cocaine use. If that euphoric, dizzying sense of exhilaration wasn't enough to make your head spin, Julio has also taken the liberty of preparing you a norepinephrine chaser to make your heart pound and breath quicken. Your infatuation experience is heightened as you start to bring about a whole new level of focus to your beloved object of desire.

But Julio's work is far from done. Serotonin, our mood regulator, plummets, causing us to obsess over our romance. Now we've entered the stage of I-can't-eat-or-sleep-God-you're-great-can't-get-you-out-of-my-head lunacy of infatuation. The part of our brain responsible for our obsessive behavior is, according to Dr. Fisher, considered the reptilian core. A basic system closely linked with the brain's reward system, longing, motivation, extreme focus, and craving.

Dr. Fisher concludes romantic love, one of the most powerful sensations on earth, has all the hallmarks of addiction. We crave more and more of the desired person. We experience withdrawal when the object of our infatuation is not available to us. Like addiction, romantic love has the potential for relapse. Just when you think you're finally getting a grip and putting Jerk-a-Saurus-Rex behind you, a random song plays reminding you of your beloved. Instantly you are right back where you were, pining uncontrollably for the one person you cannot have. Romantic, passionate love can completely derail your ability to reason and increases your capacity for illogical decision-making … sound familiar?

So why on earth do we allow ourselves to get so carried away with such nonsense?

Because it feels so damn good.

The best part of feeling really excited about somebody is discovering their excitement for us. Being on the receiving end of Julio's charms feels euphoric. As Robert Frost said, "Love is an irresistible desire to be irresistibly desired." We love ourselves with great ease when we are looking into the mirror a new partner is holding up for us. When we are chosen by another, we feel special. We can rewrite the story of who we are. We feel validated. Someone else finds us interesting, attractive, sexy or funny. It is the grandest validation of the human experience to be seen and found desirable.

Our spirits are lifted, our senses are sharpened. We feel motivated and driven. Perhaps this is one of the biggest reasons for infidelity. Affairs are a potent tonic to counter the mundane, and silence the questions, "Am I enough?" "Is this enough?" "Will I ever feel anything ever again?" It isn't difficult to imagine the turmoil that can result when partners are relating to each other unconsciously, going through the motions of life and then cross paths with someone who ignites long forgotten desires.

These themes of discontent within exclusive relationships are what sparked decades of research by Belgian psychotherapist, author, and speaker, Esther Perel. She examines the tipping point of contentment in human relationships as the pendulum swings between the need for security and autonomy. One of Perel's most revealing discoveries comes from her body of work in her book *The State of Affairs: Rethinking Infidelity*. She suggests, "When we are drawn by the gaze of another, it has less to do with wanting to be with someone else as it does with wanting to be someone else."

The elation that is experienced during infatuation tricks us into believing that we have finally met *the right one*. This myth of the "right person" is one of the biggest dysfunctional belief systems of our society. "Mr. Right" lies at the root of your unhappiness. As a child, Disney misled you. As an adolescent, Hollywood stepped in to continue the ruse. As an adult, you were subconsciously primed to believe in grandiose ideas about love and romance that come to us through movies, songs, and books. This sets the stage for the restlessness to find that special person who you know in your heart you deserve. When opportunity strikes, you're a sitting duck for Julio's charms. A few years down the road the glow wears off. You realize you and your partner don't complete each other after all. The search is on again.

The right person is about as real as Santa Claus or the Easter Bunny. We have the ability to be happy with any number of people with whom we are compatible. When I say compatible, I don't mean that you both like to do goat yoga on a paddleboard at seven in the morning. I am talking about the big stuff. Do you share a similar credence? Do you both want to raise a litter of kids or be a professional couple and shack up in a kick-ass condo? Are you intellectual equals? Can you work toward a common goal for the future? Can you find humor in your differences? Do you both have the capacity for compassion, introspection, and forgiveness?

Those last ones are huge. I can't think of any other traits that serve two people better throughout the battlefield of time. Remaining *in love* with someone once Julio's infatuation shooters have worn-off involves daily, conscious choice. We have to choose to be in love with our partners, again and again.

This is as sexy and exciting as eating Jell-O by candlelight while doing your taxes, but the fact remains these initial emotions (or should I say reactions?) causing us to pursue our attractions have absolutely NOTHING to do with loving someone authentically. Our initial stirrings that carry us on the wings of love's ethos are born from the alchemy of the brain's fluctuating chemicals. Now read that last sentence again and take a minute to let it sink in. This revelation is sad and sobering but also empowering.

Our heads are so fueled by false notions of what love and sex should be. We become crippled by narcissistic longings, searching for the one who will make us happy. While we're caught up in this cycle we will never find that person. We're too busy searching for the person we feel we deserve — those ethereal creatures who will reflect back what we desperately want to see; somebody worthy of love. It sounds like a good plan in theory but there's a fly in the Chardonnay —when you are constantly looking for yourself in the eyes of another, you will always remain lost.

The inability to truly love someone is a direct result of the inability to love yourself. Secure people do not need a partner to hold up a mirror with a flattering image. They seek relationships for other reasons; to build and share their lives. They look for someone who is available to share intimacy and companionship.

Like all drugs, the buzz of love will decline. When that rosy glow of initial infatuation passes many of us realize we have committed ourselves to someone who frustrates us, doesn't understand us, makes irrational demands of us, and is our polar opposite —thanks a lot, Julio.

Jerk.

I was bitterly disappointed when this revelation landed in my own marriage. I felt cheated, abandoned and angry. Our relationship had been tested. The buzz of our perfect romance failed to shield us from the realities of marriage: the exhaustion of rearing a family, the pressure of household finances and being responsible adults with the demands of two children and two careers.

Our conversations no longer centered around George Lucas films, take-out cuisine, or the expansion of the universe. Instead, we fought over what to do with our two-and-a-half-year-old who wasn't speaking, the baby who wasn't sleeping, the cat that wasn't pooping in its litterbox, and the household debt that was continuing to rise.

This is the part where there is no help whatsoever from Julio and his sex-on-the-beach cocktails. All the lustful yearnings we once held for our partners now serve us as well as a teapot that has its handle and spout on the same side.

Julio has left the building.

God, I hate that guy.

Now we play the blame-and-shame game. We point fingers at our partner when we're submerged in a cycle of stress and dissatisfaction. We judge our partner's shortcomings and quietly cultivate an attitude of scathing disappointment. We start to piece together the puzzle as if in a game of *Clue*, to arrive at the conclusion that our misery lies at the hands of our spouse. *Aha! It was Colonel Mustard, leaving his socks all over the study, forgetting to pick up the kids again and not supporting my Etsy shop…that's why I'm miserable! That bastard!*

We swear up and down to ourselves, and perhaps to others, we would never have entered into commitment with our partners had we known their true natures. We fail to understand really knowing someone is a slow-burning process requiring years of situations to work through.

But we pound our fists, insisting if we had the chance to go back and do it over again, we wouldn't make the same mistakes. We'd choose our partner more wisely. Many of us leave. We shuffle the deck again and start over with someone new. Of course, some of us won't leave. We choose to sink deeper into a complacent existence of misery and loathing.

But we can choose differently. We can choose to admit we are flawed, and we've chosen to build a life with another flawed individual. We can take ownership of the portion of unhappiness we have brought to the table. We can accept with compassion the flaws of our partners and not make them responsible for our well-being. We can look for things to appreciate about them. We can provide our support in times of struggle. If the best way to honor ourselves and our partners is to move on from the relationship, we can separate in love and make the choice to leave bitterness out of the equation.

Not every relationship is meant to last a lifetime, including those that revolve around mortgage payments and child-rearing. But every relationship holds the potential for growth. Relationships shine light on our strengths as well as our weaknesses. They show us our character, flaws, and our vulnerabilities. As the years roll by we inevitably find ways to step on each other's toes and stick our fingers in old wounds. Then one day, we realize our partners are no longer the energizing source of vitality they once were. We feel drained by them to the point of not liking ourselves when we are in their company. This our grandest opportunity for personal growth.

The gift of introspection is both beautiful and awful. Acknowledging your demons and admitting the negative effect they have on your life and the lives of others is a grinding endeavor. Personal growth, as it unfolds in real-time, almost always sucks. A powerful thing occurs when a couple commits themselves to doing this kind of work together.

They link hands and pull the load forward. The burden is relieved. They reinforce (if not flat-out replace) the foundation of their relationship with a newly strengthened bedrock that is strong and flexible in a way it was not before. They learn how to handle differences, negotiate sore subjects and work toward their common goals as a team. They relearn the value of respecting one another's individuality while securing the bond of the couple.

If at the end of such an undertaking the couple decide the relationship cannot move forward, then two people are given the gift of parting company without the ghosts of unfinished business haunting them in their next relationship. If they choose to remain together, they will have learned an important lesson on how to work on building the love that will sustain them for many years to come. A couple's perseverance to continue working on themselves and their relationship forges the much-envied true love many of us long to experience.

Marriage is far from being the finish line. It is the beginning of a union of life-altering consequences for both partners, regardless of how long it lasts. You will not remain the same people who originally entered the union. Whether your pairing is bound by religious, civil, or common-law union, it will not be immune from hardship. No relationship is unbreakable. Love demands work.

Of course, we don't think of these things when we're caught up in the rush of gazing into a new partner's eyes or the pleasure of a day at the spa with our bridal party to prepare for our upcoming wedding. We don't consider the consequences of our pairing while having the last dress fitting before the big day. We don't realize that the true work is just beginning.

This is what I am reminded of as I sift through my discomfort brought upon by the strolling couple. The initial and most pleasurable rush of infatuation may be gone, but it has been replaced by something far more sustainable that is not dependent on Julio's happy hour.

Today, and every day that follows, my husband and I consciously choose to be with each other. Sometimes we need to stop and take notice of what we have instead of what we wish we had. Despite the beauty and purity of the early stages of romantic love, we all come to realize the truth behind the words of the French writer, poet, and aviator, Antoine de Saint-Exupéry, "Love is not just looking at each other, it's looking in the same direction."

COMING HOME

"I love my house, I love my nest, in all the world my nest is best."
—Mr. Bird from P.D. Eastman's The Best Nest

This month, my family is celebrating an important anniversary. It is the fifteenth year that we have been living in our home. Fifteen years of building our dreams and ambitions under one roof. I remember the thrill of visiting the construction site, the anticipation to move in and start our family, even the way we romanticized the mundane tasks of homeownership. This wood and brick structure that was going up bit by bit in front of our eyes was the carrier of our hopes and dreams. It would singlehandedly ferry us into happiness.

TAKE A CLOSER LOOK...

During our home's construction, we allowed ourselves to get carried away with excitement and view the house as something that would bring us happiness. Perhaps that is why we eventually become disillusioned with the place where we hang our hats at the end of the day. Once the novelty and euphoria had worn off, we began to compare what we have with what others possess. In our neighborhood, there are trendy, stacked condos, lovely townhomes, even lovelier single-family homes and the grandiose three-car-garage homes with immaculate upgrades. My husband and I both come from modest backgrounds. When we first moved into our house, it felt lavish. Not one, but two bathrooms! I enjoyed the task of feathering our new nest and feeling the success of my official arrival into adulthood. But the more familiar we became with our neighborhood, the more our perspective began to change. Suddenly, the idea of being attached at the garage or sharing a driveway with a neighbor felt like an inconvenience. We had been invited to the Joneses' house for an evening of entertainment and we left feeling the desire to keep up.

NOW ADJUST YOUR PERSPECTIVE...

Just as depression distorts your mind to see negativity, being surrounded by grandiose houses distorts your perception of what you require to live comfortably and contentedly. This was never more poignant than when a longtime friend from my hometown came to visit. I had to suppress a chuckle when he complimented my house's loveliness. My reaction was to dismiss the compliment because I lived in a little townhouse. Even as I write this, I want to give myself a good, hard smack. When I first moved into this "little" house, I thought it was the coziest, most beautiful place I had ever seen. Now I considered myself a resident of some obscure, tiny home in a suburban ghetto.

First World problems. Good thing I'm tough.

A few years ago, after we ceased an attempt to move into a larger house I started looking at my home with fresh eyes. I felt a deep-seated appreciation for the history my family had written within its walls. Instead of seeing an old, outdated breakfast bar, I saw the nook that had given me a great place to roll out pastry as well an ideal place to change an infant and house baby supplies. This sunny, southeast-facing corner of my home served as a cradle of inspiration providing my children with a large, flat area to draw and paint, and a warm, inviting refuge for me to sit and write.

Instead of being frustrated by my house's small entrance, I transformed the walk-in hall closet into a mini-mudroom. We renovated the basement. We built a deck in the backyard. (Okay, technically, my sister and her husband built a deck in our backyard, but I watched attentively.)

Little by little, we became invested once again in our house, giving it that wonderful feeling that is known as "home."

WHAT IS A HOME?

While the words *house* and *home* are synonymous, for me the word *house* refers to the physical structure of the building, while the word *home* relates to all the sentimental value that we attach to it.

Home is a feeling.

It's where you belong and are most at ease. It's that spot on the couch where you always sit. It's that favorite teacup that you always use. It's the pile of pillows on the floor of your daughter's closet where she sits to read her comic books and writes the word *poo* on the walls. It's the Lego X-Wing on top of your mantelpiece that's a reminder of the Christmas morning your husband and son built it while consuming an entire Terry's Chocolate Orange. It's your return from a long day to the smell of something great cooking in the kitchen. It's the relief as your feet slide into the coolness of your sheets and you succumb to sleep. Whether you live in a yurt, apartment or a mansion, the feeling of being at home is something that has absolutely nothing to do with the size or appearance of your dwelling. It has to do with the emotions you invest in it. When you no longer infuse your living accommodations with the feelings of connectedness, you will no longer be happy living there. If you want to *feel* at home, you must *be* at home — not daydreaming about how much better your life would be if you had more.

That is a game not easily won.

Presently, we are comfortable and confident that our house is able to give us everything we require. As the weather continues to warm up, I find my thoughts drifting to the backyard and playing in the dirt, preparing the garden, adding some perennial beds, all of these are activities I associate with one of my favorite places to be in the summer.

I smile as I think of this, immersed in my task of icing our home's birthday cake (never waste a golden opportunity to eat cake, kids.) Tonight at dinner, we will eat cake and reminisce over pictures of our house's construction. When my husband eyes me suspiciously and asks what we are celebrating, I will respond with "fifteen years of great memories, and many more to come."

MAMA KNOWS BEST…

THE GOOD MOTHER

An open letter to mothers everywhere who are in the all-consuming early years.

"There's no way to be a perfect mother and a million ways to be a good one."—Jill Churchill

Hey Mama,

I wanted you to know that I noticed you today in line at the grocery store. I saw the dark circles under your eyes, the frantic search in your purse for your keys and heard the sharp tone in your voice when you spoke to your children. I saw how you struggled to get the groceries into your car as you simultaneously tried to prevent your toddler from running into parking-lot traffic. I saw how difficult it was to get those flailing, chubby little arms into the car seat. I saw that look on your face as you tried to ignore the tantrum of your older daughter because you would not buy her that chocolate bar.

We don't know each other by name, but we certainly know the life that each is living. At times this life brings incredible joy and at others, incredible difficulty. It's so difficult I sometimes find myself wishing I could just walk away from it. I thought maybe there was a chance you felt the same way. Perhaps, late at night you say something like that to yourself and spend the next several days hating yourself for it. It is easy to feel as if all the mamas around you have it put together so much better than you do. They eat better, live tidier, meet all their deadlines and do it with clean clothes and manicured hands. They don't live like we do. No, Ma'am. We come barreling down the grocery store aisle like a drunken Grizzly bear with an infant strapped to our chest who smells like he's fermenting in his own juices and a toddler yelling at the top of his lungs. It is the second trip we have made to the grocery store today. We couldn't remember all the things we needed the first time around. Things get a little fuzzy when your day begins at 2 am and finishes at 12:45 am. That's how *we* roll. The truly unfortunate thing now is we're in the frozen food section. You know how much we hate the frozen food section, right? Every time that damned glass door slams shut we get an eyeful of the disheveled, scattered mess we've become. As we come face to face with the stranger standing in our shoes desperately trying to keep it together, we can't help but wonder what the real problem is. Is it my kids, or is it me?

    Self-loathing is hard work, Mama. This kind of

job quickly becomes a lifestyle. I have made earnest efforts to extricate myself from this line of work and go into early retirement. Sadly, the powers that be at Self-Loathing Inc. are a relentless bunch, and they feel that my presence is greatly needed. Perhaps they are trying to recruit you as well? I've done some background checking and I want to let you know that they are *not* registered with the Better Business Bureau. Their wages leave much to be desired and their benefits package sucks. Last spring, I handed them my third (and hopefully final) letter of resignation. I am currently pursuing a management position with a few other places. Maybe you've heard of them?

Cut-Myself-Some-Freaking-Slack Inc.;

I'm-Doing-The-Best-I-Can Inc.;

Quit-Trying-To-Be-So-Damn Perfect Inc.

Currently, I am filling a contract position at Margaritaville Inc., but it's only a temporary position that will be over by summer's end.

Shame … it's a pretty sweet gig.

Today I want to let you know that when I saw you, I saw a good mom who was having a bad day. No matter what happened today, you loved your children. You fed them, clothed them and when they smelled bad enough, you gave them a bath.

You are doing a good job.

Maybe you lost your cool today for a little while and yelled at your three-year-old. Maybe you've eaten grilled cheese sandwiches for supper every night this week because your teething baby wouldn't give you time to get anything else together.

You are still doing a good job.

Maybe your house looks like a cyclone ran through it. You've been wearing the same shirt for three days. You haven't had more than four or five hours of broken sleep a night in the last eighteen months. You and your husband haven't had a night out together since the Obama administration.

Did it sink in when I said you were doing a good job?

No? Fine. I'll say it again.

You, Mama, are doing a good job.

Your house isn't perfect. Your marriage isn't perfect. Your children aren't perfect. You look around and see that you have everything you've ever wanted, yet at times all you feel is exhausted and miserable. (Psst … come and see me at Margaritaville Inc. I've got something that can help you with this.)

I can let you in on a little secret. You don't have to be living a perfect existence to be a good mom. It is okay to be a "good enough" mom. This idea you have in your head that's pushing you to perform this stage of parenting better is never going to be within your grasp. It doesn't exist. Facebook and Instagram would have us believe otherwise but the truth is the fiercest among us are still running around in the same yoga pants we've been wearing for the last five business days. Your neighbor has just posted a picture that shows her and her preschooler making puff pastry in a spotless kitchen with the caption #mamalife. That's beautiful. Truly, but don't let it get you down. Consider posting your own mama pic with a selfie of you wearing a big smile because you got to pee in the bathroom alone for the first time in three weeks. Casually mention you decided to pamper yourself by brushing your teeth. Insert raise-the-roof emoji here. Do not forget to stage the photo. This is very important. We want to reach the masses here. For maximum effect, make sure to have a few prescription bottles of Zoloft or Prozac in the background; and don't forget to add some pinecones. People cannot get enough of that shit. They just make everything feel warm and homey, don't they? Now choose the perfect hashtag: #reallife. Get ready, my friend. You're about to become a major influencer.

Now let's cut the crap. These early years are the hard, hard work of mothering. They wear on you, chipping away little pieces of your soul and sanity each day. If you aren't careful, there won't be anything left of you to enjoy the beautiful moments of motherhood when your heart feels full; you'll feel like a helium balloon floating in the sky.

Look at your children, Mama. They are alive. They are healthy. They are good, especially that one with the marker in his hand who has climbed to the top of the kitchen pantry. Maybe consider gymnastics camp? Just a thought.

Listen to me, tired, hard-working Mama. It gets better. They get older. You start getting more sleep at night. They start wiping their own backsides. Lingering bubble baths, nights out with friends, hobbies and reading books with no pictures or rhyming text in them, these are all going to come back.

Maybe right now all you need is to take a leave of absence from Self-Loathing Inc. It's okay to admit to someone else that you are having a hard time and would like some help. It's the first, important step in improving your current circumstances. You don't feel like this because you're a bad mom. You feel like this because it's damn tough right now. You've got some major physiological and emotional needs not being met right now. All of us are struggling. Some of us just hide it better. Not you and I, though. We wear our hearts on our sleeves. Right next to the spit-up and coffee stains. Now is not the time to berate yourself for not thriving. You are in survival mode, soldier. In order to survive, you keep putting one foot in front of the other until you make it to the other side. I'll be waiting for you at base camp. Play your cards right and I'll have a little V.I.P package from Margaritaville Inc., waiting for you too.

Oh, and before I forget … you are a good mom.

DEAR DAUGHTER

There is nothingas powerful as a mothers love, and nothing as healing as a child's soul.

I am sitting at my computer, discreetly munching on the chocolate bunny I have hidden from the rest of my family. My purpose today is to consider my ever-evolving relationship with a significant young woman in my life: my daughter. Since I am a woman writing a book for other women, I want to evaluate what it means to be a mother to a daughter and what I hope to show her while raising her.

My daughter and I are currently locking horns over just about everything. I write these narratives directly to her so that someday, perhaps when she is older, she will read this and gain some insight about her crazy artist mother's thought processes and how fiercely she was loved.

Dear Daughter (April 2008):

Today is a day so filled with joy, my heart wants to explode. Your father and I have just come home from a prenatal ultrasound appointment, riding high from the news we're carrying a girl. A girl!

Ever since I was old enough to play with dolls, I yearned to be a mother to a daughter. I imagined all the tea parties we would attend together, the crafts we would do and how much fun it would be to teach you how to bake cookies. I close my eyes and try to picture what you will look like. What will you take from me? Will you have my eyes? My hair color? Will we have the same laugh? Will you also be an artist? I am so excited to meet you that I regularly take out your ultrasound picture and try out the names we are thinking of giving to you. Olivia, Francesca, Laura … they all have a rolling, feminine lilt that is so much more pleasing on the tongue than Cletus-the-fetus (that was all your dad's idea, sorry).

Everywhere I go, the color pink stands out to me. I have already started collecting baby clothes in shades of pink and lavender. I also have a box in my closet that contains little bobbles and barrettes, because if you're anything like me and your aunties, you'll have TONS of hair. I've already got your dress picked out for your first birthday party. In fact, I've got the entire template of our lives all sketched out and ready to go, like some well-planned story outline. All I need to do is just pop in the characters.

I don't yet realize this, but as of this moment, I am making YOUR life all about ME. Your impending debut into the world feels like it is something that is happening to me. It's another chapter in my own story and I just can't wait to write it. While my perspective may be a little narrow at the moment, I can tell you without reservation that everything I am doing in the months leading up to meeting you for the first time is done out of a desire to give you the best life possible.

Already, you have made me proud.

Already, I consider myself the luckiest mother on the planet.

Already, I love you to the moon and back.

Dear Daughter (November 2012):

You are so small as I write this to you, still content to hold hands with me on our travels. The fading warmth of your palm in mine, a considerable reminder that these sweet days are numbered.

My baby is gone. You have now become your own little person, funny and headstrong, curious about everything. I watch as you throw yourself headfirst into life with trademark four-year-old gusto.

I feel a range of emotions I did not know were possible to feel for another human being. You have opened my heart in ways that delight, overwhelm, and ground me into the things that matter most.

Though your arrival into my life was not without its complications, I thank you for the patience you showed me as I struggled to regain my sense of balance, waiting with open arms to welcome me as your mother.

In many ways, I am learning just as much as you about the world around us. Being your mother has reflected back to me my own strengths and weaknesses. It has shown me who I am and who I want to be. Often, I am concerned that I am not mothering you correctly and that my shortcomings will have a negative impact on you. I have made it my mission to make sure that I am present for you in every aspect of your life. I have made your happiness MY RESPONSIBILITY and have vowed not to let you down.

I don't yet realize this, but your happiness isn't actually something that is within my control. MY life is all about YOU right now, and I haven't yet come to terms with the reasoning that being SUPERMOM isn't what you need from me. In fact, if anything, it's impeding your independence and growth and leaving you with a worn-out and irritable parent. My bad, Peanut, not yours.

Please hang in there with me a little while longer. I'm just beginning to quiet all the noise in my head and am coming to grasp the concept of what my role in our lives should be. I foresee a lot of improvement in my future disposition.

In any case, however many bumps we hit in the road along the way, I want you to know a few things:

I am so proud of you.

I am the luckiest mother on the planet.

I love you to the moon and back.

Dear Daughter (August 2019):

How is it the days have seemed endless, yet the years have sped by? I can hardly believe my eyes on some days, watching you walk in the door after school. My little girl is gone now, too. Safely tucked away in the archives of digital photos with the baby who has also left, you now stand on the cusp of becoming a teenager.

You are not shy about disagreeing with me, more often than I care to admit. You have your own opinions and your own way of doing things, which is completely different from mine. We are unalike in many ways. Your introversion perplexes me. My extraversion embarrasses you. Your personal style of organization irritates me to no end. My need for order is stifling for you. We tend to stick our fingers in each other's sore spots a lot lately, posturing about the house, locked in our mutual power struggle.

On some days, we go back and forth from snippy engagements to the silent treatment. And still, no matter how irritable our exchanges are during the day, you seek me out in the evenings to slide under my arm and ask if we can read together. Sometimes you want me to read you a chapter, and other times you want to read to me and share a paragraph of something you found totally hilarious. One thing we do have in common is a zany and somewhat off-color sense of humor accompanied by a penchant for practical jokes. I promise to help you reel that one in and learn to use it appropriately (just as soon as I've finished learning how to do that for myself, of course).

Sadly, you no longer want to hold my hand when we're out but you're still game to help out in the kitchen, especially if I agree to let you lick the spatula and look the other way when you steal chocolate chips from the bag. I listen as you speak with animation about all the interesting facts about animal biology you read in National Geographic. You are one part artist, one part scientist, and one hundred percent yourself.

Physically, you look like your dad's side of the family. Then I take notice of your love for art, books and how skillfully you saran-wrapped the toilet seat a few months back, and I can see some of me in there, too.

I am just beginning to see that we are, and will always be, separate people. It was never your job to be an extension of me. It was never my job to tell you what to think or make you behave in a way that was comforting to me. My job is to provide for your needs and teach you how to provide for your wants. I am to be your moral compass until you figure out how to get your own needle spinning. I am to provide support without rescue, compassion without co-dependence and show you how important it is to love yourself. The truth of the matter is you and your brother don't really "belong" to me. You may be my kids, but you are your own people. What people really need in life is love, acceptance, and guidance. That means I have to let you take the lead more often even if that makes me uncomfortable. This is how people learn. This is how children become adults. I will work hard to do better here, even if that means causing upset between us.

I have also noticed how less than impressed you are with my absence due to work or my need to flee to a quiet place to write. You asked me once how it was I claimed to enjoy spending time with you when I am always so busy. While the sight of your pouty grimace when I leave for work still pierces me in the gut, I have made the choice to continue being engaged in my work teaching dance and writing because they both bring a lot of joy and fulfillment to my life.

I am just beginning to figure out that by not pursuing my own passions, I am leaving you with a joyless parent who is experiencing some major deficits in the mental health department. That is a pain I am taking great care not to impress upon you and your brother. Even though you snicker when you see me practicing dance steps or get excited about skiing, you are also observing someone who is committed to creating joy in her life. A joyful woman can be a joyful mother. Joyful mothers make some of the best parents out there, and that's what I want for you, Pussycat.

It's a lot to take in right now. I get that. But perhaps one day you will become a mother yourself and will really understand what I mean when I tell you:

I am so proud of you.

I am the luckiest mother on the planet.

I love you to the moon and back.

A HAT OF ONE'S OWN

"The joys of motherhood are never fully experienced until the children are in bed."—Unknown

When a woman enters motherhood, she becomes the proprietor of an extensive collection of hats she will wear over the course of her lifetime. Being a mother means she will at times wear the *nurture hat*, kissing all the boo-boos and tucking in all the toes at bedtime. She may also have to wear her *warrior hat*, doing battle with the obstacles standing in the way of her child's rights. Sometimes she must face the demands of an unsympathetic teacher. At other times she must demonstrate how to draw a line in the sand to stop a bully. Some mothers are called upon to wage war against an invisible enemy who resides inside the neurology of her child, causing daily struggles, difficult behaviors, and general discord.

She will wear her *teacher, playmate, nurse, chauffeur* and *therapist hat;* possibly all at the same time. She will be so many things to her children over the course of their formative years, it's no wonder she can easily become disconnected from herself. Rapidly changing hats runs the risk of losing the one you originally wore to the party in the first place.

The connection we have to our identity is a powerful tether that keeps our spirit whole. It allows us to experience the joy in life. When motherhood comes into our lives, we are thrown into an all-consuming role like a raging fire. This can result in the abandonment of joys we created for ourselves prior to our child's arrival.

I remember in my pre-baby days I would see those advertisements for Johnson & Johnson baby shampoo. They depicted a lovely scene of a woman giving her cooing infant a bath in the kitchen sink. The tagline for this commercial was *Having a baby changes everything.* The woman was happy. The baby was happy. It all looked so good.

Sign me up! I'm in!

It was a year into the motherhood gig when I realized that having a baby does indeed change everything. But not every change feels like a change for the better: constant exhaustion, prolonged sleep deprivation and the unrelenting responsibility for the survival of this tiny person who is completely dependent on you. None of us are prepared for how hard this is. The desperate aching in our bones for self-care gets deferred, sometimes at great cost to our physical, mental and emotional health. At a time when we should be showing ourselves the most compassion, we are harsh and unkind. We wonder why we can't be happy in our role as a twenty-four-hour dairy delivery service. We have arrived at motherhood's doorstep with the idea that this is our grandest purpose in life.

Why aren't we happy? What's wrong with us? We must be terrible people.

Part of the issue may lie with the twenty-first-century culture of child-rearing. I once asked my aunt, who married at the age seventeen and had five children, if she was happy during her child-rearing years. She responded with a noncommittal shrug and told me that she never really had time to think about it. It took all of her and my uncle's time and resources to provide shelter, food, and clothing for their family. Getting everybody's needs met equaled success for them.

My generation was raised differently. We were told from a young age that we were special and could do anything we wanted. Girls, as well as boys, were encouraged to pursue their passions and become educated. Young marriages became the exception rather than the norm. Young women postponed marriage until after post-secondary education. Many continued to postpone it further until they established careers. This resulted in years of a person creating their self-identity. Women today construct their adult lives building their careers while cultivating interests and hobbies. Then, one day, fueled by strong biological urges, along with a slew of social half-truths, we come to motherhood with the somewhat mistaken belief that this will make us happy.

We are trained to believe we can have it all, and this is a big piece of it. The life we once had comes crashing down as Humpty Dumpty takes his tumble off the wall. Like shattered eggs shells in our palms, there's just no putting it back together. The person we were comes to a grinding halt as a new identity takes shape.

I am Mommy. Hear me roar.

When we realize perhaps being somebody's mother won't bring about a sense of wholeness, after all, it throws us into a spiral of guilt and despair.

Here's what I know: motherhood is not a quick sprint. It is a marathon that requires serious endurance. If any woman is to experience happiness in motherhood she must first find it within herself. She must surround herself with the things and people that nurture her spirit. When we show ourselves love we are able to offer more of it to the people who matter most in our lives. We must put careful thought into what nurtures us and wisely design a hat of our own that reflects our authentic selves. Each woman's hat will be made of different material, but they are usually constructed from; laughter, female companionship, the pursuit of interests outside of child-rearing, time with their partner and the precious commodity of solitude.

It's a simple equation that can seem difficult to work out. But it bears repeating, again and again. The more you nurture yourself the better you will be able to nurture your children. The kindest thing you can do for them is be kind to yourself. For your children to grow up loving and accepting themselves; you must model love and acceptance of yourself.

They are watching us. They are paying attention. What do you want to show them? An exhausted and miserable role model with a dozen hats stacked precariously on her head? Or a confident and content leader with a firm grasp on the most important hat in her collection – her true self. When we wear that hat around our family members we're in a position to offer something good and make a worthy impact in their lives. So go dig yours up, would you? If you can't find it, make a new one. Then hang onto it with everything you've got.

SLOW YOUR ROLL

RUNNING ON EMPTY

"The definition of insanity is doing the same thing over and over again but expecting different results."
—*Albert Einstein*

When I was younger I was terrible at reading and responding to signs. I was so narrowly focused on what I was doing I refused to pay attention to what was happening around me. This little deficit of mine caused me to fall victim to my own stupidity repeatedly. The following is an excerpt from the chronicles of Dumb-Assery.

Allow me to set the stage...

Picture it: North Bay, Ontario, 1993. The heroine of our story (btw, that's me), a high-school senior, is late for her school's pancake breakfast fundraiser. Still wearing pajamas (the chosen attire for all pancake chefs), she jumps into a 1985 Hyundai Pony, complete with manual choke (go ahead, it's okay to be jealous) and races to school. The fuel light had lit up two days before and alerted our heroine her chariot required refueling. Being the busy young lady that she is, she thinks *I'll get to that later.* This results in the car coming to a sputtering stop halfway to her destination.

What a plot twist! Who could have seen that one

coming, right?

Armed with a spatula and mixing bowl, our frustrated heroine boldly charges out on foot into the snow (btw, it's February in this story), clad in her sleepwear and fetches a jerry can of fuel at a nearby gas station. The smart choice would be to drive immediately to the gas station for a proper fill-up. Alas, our young heroine at this time is still somewhat naïve. She chooses to continue driving to school, making no unnecessary stops except for the bank, corner store and then the drugstore. This results in the car running out of fuel for a second time on her way home.

Fortunately, lady luck is on her side as she finds herself yet again within walking distance to a gas station to fetch *another* jerry can of gas. Strangely, it is, in fact, the same gas station she had visited earlier with the same cashier. But even at the tender age of seventeen-and-three-quarters, our heroine has a remarkable capacity for handling such matters. She cleverly disguises her identity by reversing her jacket and donning a pair of sunglasses. It should be noted that the sunglasses happen to be a novelty trinket leftover from the prizes that were doled out that morning at the fundraiser and are ridiculously oversized and covered in sparkly palm trees. But if anyone can pull off this look in the middle of winter, it's her. This time our heroine slowly peruses the offerings in the convenience aisles and brings an eclectic array of items to the counter; sports beverages, feminine hygiene products, and trail mix. When the nice lady at the cash register asks her if she needs anything else today, our heroine stoically adjusts her eyewear and responds with a nonchalant, "Yes, would you happen to sell jerry cans?"

"Oh, my Lord," the nice lady replies, "you ran out of gas *again?!?*"

It would appear the cashier possesses freakish super-human X-ray vision and sees right through our heroine's disguise. She recognizes the frazzled young lady with the frozen hair who is still wearing her pajamas this late afternoon. But do not despair! Our mercurial heroine, who is blessed to be born under the sign of Gemini, is nothing if not quick thinking. She looks the counter attendant in the eye and explains she has a twin sister who routinely neglects to fuel up the shared vehicle.

Well done, Lucy.

In my present-day life, I have proudly learned to avoid the unpleasant consequence of running out of gas by responding to my car's fuel gauge. Unfortunately, I have not done so well recognizing and responding to the signs that my own tank requires refueling. My warning signs include; difficulty concentrating, forgetfulness, feeling scattered, insomnia, low energy and an impending feeling of resentment toward anyone who comes at me with the phrase, "Hey, can you…"

Spring is one of the toughest times of year for me.

The return of longer days and warmer weather forewarns my collapse into debilitating fatigue. I find it extremely difficult to cope with my life and the people in it. This leads to feelings of unworthiness and self-loathing. I become a glorious recipe for misery.

The great thing about recognizing and responding to exhaustion is by prioritizing our own needs we are better equipped to care for the people who rely on us the most. Truly, it makes little difference whether we organize the clutter in January or June. Pushing ourselves until we end up in the fetal position does little to serve anybody around us. It also sets up our children for spectacular failure as adults if this is the model we provide. The best thing we can do is teach them to care for themselves. The best way to do that is to care for you.

Learn to say, "No, I can't do that." The earth will not swallow you whole if you move those items on your list to next week, next month or next season. Make time for frivolous things like having fun. It is more important than you realize.

Our ideas of what refueling means will be different. Perhaps an evening out for Thai food and cosmos with cherished friends fills your tank. Maybe it's taking a Paint Night class. Perhaps it's making time to read a good book or listen to new music. Whatever your idea of refueling, make it happen. Pay close attention to your own dashboard. Learn to recognize and respond to the early precursors of exhaustion. Keep your tank reasonably full. Being engaged in your life with a full tank versus hopping around from place to place with a tiny jerry can in your hand will be a game-changer. Only you can make that happen for yourself.

    Your fuel is a precious resource.

    It's finite. It has to be replenished.

    Give your tank the respect it deserves.

    Fill 'em up.

THE ILLUSION OF PRODUCTIVITY

"In an age of distraction, nothing can feel more luxurious than paying attention."
—Pico Iyer, *The Art of Stillness*

I am enjoying my time alone. There is a stillness of mind on these mornings by the water. I walk with an unapologetic lack of purpose. It's so uncharacteristic I am tempted to check my reflection in the river to ensure I am really here. Usually, I am in a rush. Always on the verge of being late, usually due to trying to squeeze multiple tasks into not enough time. While I always appear to be busy and constantly feel exhausted, I am often disappointed I didn't accomplish enough. From this perspective, you would think the obvious answer would be to buckle down and do more. However, recent revelations suggest a different approach: do less.

Doing nothing doesn't come easy for me. I come from hardy stock of northern Ontario female lineage that has perpetual busy-ness bred deeply into the bones. If you are like me, then you understand far too well the pervasive need to always be doing. We sacrifice the ability to be present when we are uncomfortable with stillness. We choose to be in the company of exhaustion rather than the hostility of our unoccupied minds. We wear fatigue like a badge of honor. We take pleasure in hearing people refer to us as machines. We glorify overextension. It means we're in demand. The more in demand we are the more worthy we feel. So we continue to soldier on and attempt to defy the laws of physics by being in multiple places at once. Our smartphones allow us to be in the workplace while at home and be at home while we're at work. The constant pinging of our phones provides a spectacular recipe for distraction-induced psychosis.

We fancy ourselves to be well-seasoned multitaskers, boldly taking productivity to new heights. But our skewed perceptions of accomplishment may be little more than delusions of grandeur, according to Earl Miller, a neuroscientist at MIT who has become an expert researcher in the field of fractured attention spans.

Miller's research suggests when busy people perceive they are multitasking, their brain is really switching gears at great speed from one task to another. The cost for this rapid cognitive border crossing of neurological pathways is steep. It leads to an increase of the stress hormones cortisol and adrenaline.

Overabundance of these two chemicals has been proven to overstimulate the brain, causing mental fog and fuzzy, disjointed thinking. We've convinced ourselves this state of mind is our version of normal before receiving adequate levels of caffeine. New parents often struggle with constant interruption to basic tasks such as eating and sleeping. We only need to look at the sleep-deprived, frazzled young mother who can't find her car keys and has difficulty finishing a coherent sentence to see this theory in practice.

Chronic multitasking, combined with electronic devices creates a dopamine addiction as it trains and rewards the brain to constantly seek out external stimuli. This explains why we are so dependent upon our devices. We are so accustomed to our attention spans being divided we have lost our ability to stop, pay full attention and connect. We are incapable of being in the present moment.

Elevated stress hormones and fluctuating levels of dopamine create the perfect soil conditions for nurturing the seeds of depression and anxiety. Confusion, irritability, insomnia, heart palpitations, fatigue, restlessness, negativity, overreaction … does any of this sound familiar? This is what we harvest from a life of overstimulation and disconnection.

We deny responsibility for our moods and claim circumstances are beyond our control. Notable nineteenth-century philosopher and psychologist William James believed human beings could alter their lives by altering their attitudes. "The greatest weapon against stress is our ability to choose one thought over another." It is how we choose to respond to our circumstances rather than the circumstances themselves that shapes our moods. How on earth are we capable of getting a grip on our thoughts if we are at the mercy of some neurotoxic Kool-Aid that is produced in our heads? How can we focus on adjusting our perspectives and engage in higher thinking if we are mercilessly distracted by work, home, kids and envy of our friend's rockin' bikini-bod selfie on Instagram?

We can't. It isn't possible.

Happiness requires placing a brick in the revolving door of life's distractions and pausing long enough to invite it in. Of course, this is much easier in theory than in practice. It requires sorting true responsibilities from unnecessary distractions. I have, over the past three years, consciously set myself the task of taking the time to do absolutely nothing. I have realized how vital it is for my mental well-being to have time for solitude.

My rejuvenation from nothing almost always encompasses being outside and disconnected from all electronic devices. Whatever way I choose to spend this time, it must never involve a task. We must commit to rewiring our brains. We must stop ourselves from rewarding busyness and appreciate the calm only stillness can bring.

In stillness, I appreciate the beauty of sunsets and

firelight.

In stillness, I inhale the goodness of a tomato plant's earthy smell.

In stillness I am able to feel how truly blessed I am simply to be alive.

To feel the connectedness of it all pulsing through my veins; this is where true happiness lives. We all have the ability to access this space.

Be happy.

Be present.

Do nothing.

Have everything.

INTERVIEW WITH AN INSOMNIAC

"Nothing cures insomnia like the realization that it's time to get up."—Anonymous

"How did you sleep last night?" This is a question I am frequently asked by my husband, who is now accustomed to waking up in an empty bed. He knows the hours between midnight and 4:00 a.m. are when my mind likes to play a little game called, "We're Off to the Races."

This charming gong show goes like this: I turn the lights off after fifteen minutes or so of successfully reading myself into a coma. I turn off the lights, say goodnight and wait for sleep to claim me. After what feels like an eternity of just hovering over the edge of a steep cliff but not falling, I transition to a state of heightened alertness combined with anger and disappointment. It's like receiving my tax return.

Then the thoughts start coming in. At first, it's a slow trickle of; *Did the kids make their lunches before bed? Or I have to remember to confirm so-and-so's dentist appointment in the morning.* Then my thoughts turn their attention to my work: *Mary has no self-confidence when she dances ... how am I going to fix that? My choreography for the Saturday class is such a mess. I have to spend more time cleaning it, and speaking of clean, I really need to get to the laundry that has been piling up, and the refrigerator needs to be cleaned out, but first I should get to the basement because it's a total disaster.* I make a mental note to never meet Marie Kondo in person because she would probably drop-kick me in the groin if she ever visited.

I peek over at the time; it's now almost two in the morning. I notice a figure cloaked in the dark shadows of the corner. It is dressed in long, flowing robes and has gnarled hands and a bent neck. I haven't been drinking this evening and am not under any pharmaceutical care, though as of this moment I am seriously beginning to consider it.

It hovers over to me. I mentally kick myself for ever agreeing to watch *The Haunting of Hill House* with my husband. I silently begin pleading with this grotesque figure to leave my room. I make all sorts of promises to it that I know I won't keep. I even point frantically at the sleeping body beside me: *Please ... take him instead.* But no such luck. It is here for me, and me alone. I expect that some terrible violence will ensue once it reaches my bedside, but instead, it just hands me a little folded-up piece of paper. I open the note and read the message.

Two words: *You. Suck.*

And then it's gone. I am left in the dark with my fear of inadequacy. Time for a change of scenery.

I have a ninja-like ability to tiptoe down the

stairs avoiding the creaky parts that would alert the other members of my household to my nocturnal roaming. I have mastered the ways of silently fretting about the living room in the middle of the night.

This is probably the most fruitless waste of time and energy a person can engage in. The impact of prolonged sleep deprivation wreaks havoc on a person's well-being with severity and cruelty. There is no swifter way to suck the life force out of someone. If you also suffer from this particular brand of deprivation, I urge you to make some conscious changes to your lifestyle (as well as some strong coffee.) Arm yourself with survival mode strategies.

Scientific studies show that prolonged sleep deprivation leads to an increase in mental health conditions such as depression and anxiety. With sleep issues, it's a bit of a chicken-or-the-egg scenario, difficult to know which one is the cause and which one is the effect. Adequate levels of sleep allow the body to regulate stress hormones, repair and restore physical ailments and keep the brain firing on all cylinders. Prolonged sleep deprivation puts you at greater risk of health issues such heart attack, stroke, obesity, hypertension, and inflammation, which in turn can result in cognitive impairments, memory loss, and set the stage for neurodegenerative diseases such as dementia and Alzheimer's.

You probably know all of this. You had every intention of getting some freaking Zzzs tonight, but alas, the Sandman never came for you. What's a sleepy gal with the weight of the world on her shoulders to do?

For starters, do not fall under the illusion that your fretting helps you control whatever circumstances are keeping you awake. Nor is it giving you any foresight into what may or may not happen. You are strapped into a roller coaster of an endless worrisome thought loop, nothing more. Your job is not to solve your perceived problems. Your job is break out of the loop of racing thoughts. Remember, you don't have to let your mind run the show. How do you do that, exactly?

#1. HIT THE PAUSE BUTTON

Break your cycle of racing thoughts by visualizing a hand or a stop sign in your mind. It's also helpful to verbalize your intention by actually saying "STOP" out loud. Just don't say it too loud if you're sharing a bed with someone. Not every sleeping partner is understanding about having their sleep disturbed because you started laying down the law with yourself.

#2. TAKE OUT THE TRASH

Once you have firmly yet lovingly told yourself to cut it out and quit being a gigantic wanker, the next step is to physically remove yourself from your bed and find some tools to empty your head.

You know how the kitchen garbage sometimes gets so full there just isn't any room left? The garbage starts spilling out around it making it impossible to be used in the functional manner for which it was designed. Sometimes during busy or stressful periods our minds do the exact same thing. They don't function in the higher thinking capacity for which they were designed. Instead, they become fixated on anxiety-generating thoughts played on repeat. Grab some paper and a pen or use the recording device on your phone to download every troublesome thought renting space in your head this evening. Say everything that comes to mind and do not censor anything. Take slow, deep breaths through your nose and exhale even slower out of your mouth. Visualize your thoughts as clouds leaving your body with each exhale. Repeat this process as many times as necessary until you feel physically feel lighter. Once you feel calm, write or speak the following: *I give myself permission to release my worries and go to sleep.* Say it until you believe it.

#3. REPLACE YOUR FOCUS

Now shift your focus on to something else. Sometimes, your irritation at not being able to sleep is enough to prevent you from falling asleep. If this is something you are struggling with, change how you view your insomnia. If you knew you were going to be executed by firing squad in the morning, you would probably be thankful for the extra wakeful hours. Remember you are lucky to have a heart beating in your chest and lungs that draw in air. Your safety isn't at risk and you're most likely warm and dry in a shelter full of food. Given the choice between a couple of sleepless nights or packing up your family and escaping an oppressive regime, most of you would choose to keep our First World problems. The key here, and I cannot stress this enough, is to change your focus. Things I find helpful for changing focus include listening to sleep meditations on YouTube or sleep stories on this wonderfully relaxing app called Calm. There you can listen to a variety of stories narrated in a soft tone of voice that will help you nod off. This will soothe your anxious mind on nights when it's running away. If you are also married to a computer genius, consider asking your partner to teach you the valuable life skills of counting in both binary and hex. No computer genius? No problem! Try counting backward from a thousand by seven. You will bore yourself to sleep. What you focus on isn't as important as the fact that you shift your focus off whatever is charging through your mind and keeping you awake. Once you stop paying attention to it, it ceases to have power.

#4. TWEAK YOUR ROUTINE

Having difficulty falling asleep every now and

then is normal. If you're being stood up by the Sandman on a regular basis, track your routine within the last two hours leading up to bedtime.

Avoid stimulating physical activity in the later evening hours, but do include some earlier in your day. Cut yourself off from all caffeinated beverages by two in the afternoon or sooner. Drink more water. Give herbal teas a whirl. Chamomile and spearmint is a wonderful tea to have in the evening and gives you that comfy *day is done* kind of feeling.

Turn the lights down low in your rooms. Have a hot shower or soak in the tub with Epsom salts before bed. Try adding some essential oils to the water. Both eucalyptus and lavender are known for their ability to induce relaxation. Make sure you dress lightly. A drop in body temperature will make you feel sleepy. Reading in bed is also a good practice to help make the eyelids heavy as long as it isn't from a brightly lit screen. Screen time on a personal device near bedtime is a nasty sleep sucker. The bright light shining into your eyes tells your body to suppress its production of melatonin, the hormone your body manufactures that regulates your sleep. If you are inclined to give any of the above sleep mediations a try make sure you are doing so with eyes closed and not looking at the screen. If you can't fall asleep, you may wish to experiment with melatonin supplements. They are available over the counter without prescription and are not habit-forming. Magnesium before bed is another recommended sleep-inducer and has the added benefit of no grogginess in the morning.

While it pains me to be the bearer of bad news, that glass of vino you may be using to unwind after a long day is probably doing more harm to your sleep. Studies have proven alcohol inhibits the body's ability to regulate its circadian rhythm, disrupting your ability to fall and stay asleep. If that glass of wine is consumed too close to bedtime, you may experience a delayed onset of sleep. If you do manage to fall asleep, your body will spend the first part of the night metabolizing the alcohol in deeper, slow-wave sleep and have less time in the restorative REM sleep that regulates mental functioning, memory, and emotional processing. REM sleep is what allows us to wake up feeling well-rested.

During the second half of the night, the sedative effects of alcohol disappear faster than your college boyfriend when you asked him to meet your parents. You experience what scientists call the "rebound effect" and can lead to disruptive flow of sleep and oh-so-early morning waking (think between three and five). The best time of day to consume alcohol is the traditional cocktail hours of 5:00 to 7:00 p.m. Swap that nightcap for a glass of wine with your meal or consider skipping it altogether for a few nights. Put on your scientist's lab coat and conduct some experiments. See what changes to your routine have the greatest effect on your sleep.

5#. SEEK HELP

If you are still not seeing any relief, I urge you to see your doctor. Sleep issues can affect your entire outlook on life and bring you down faster than figuring out your net worth. There can be a variety of health factors at play when dealing with habitual insomnia. There are treatments to tame the beast and practice better sleep hygiene to bring you the rest you need. Sleep provides us a life of thriving instead of surviving. Until then, I'll be here, brewing the coffee and the stories. Should you lean over and have a tiny nap on my shoulder, don't worry about it. I won't tell a soul.

THE ART OF PORCHING

"You find peace not by rearranging the circumstances of your life, but by realizing who you are at the deepest level."—Eckhart Tolle

When I was younger, I frequently noticed how my grandmother would spend late afternoons on the front porch of our North Bay, Ontario, home. I used to wonder what she thought about as she sat in her lawn chair, gazing at the highway that ran through our town. As a small child, I asked Granny if she was counting cars.

She gave me a little smile before answering, "Yes, I am."

I've often thought about my grandmother during calmer moments from the frenzy of my life. *How the heck did she do it back then?* I muse while ferrying children to karate and gymnastics classes. When I compare our lives, I am embarrassed to admit on most days I feel overwhelmed. I'm raising two children; she raised six. I have a home filled with modern conveniences; she had a home with a wood stove and no hot water. I have a vehicle at my disposal; she did not. When I complain about having to empty the washing machine for the third time in the same day, I think about her doing laundry for eight people with a washboard and a bar of soap.

When I put it on paper it's obvious to see there is no contest: Lucy: 0, Granny: 1,000,000. So why does it feel like my life is so damn difficult all the time?

Though it is true that women today in the developed world enjoy freedom of choice far more than ever before, I feel many of these choices also enslave us to a life of overextension and exhaustion. Just because we live with the freedom to do everything doesn't mean we should.

There is a lot to be said for living life in its simpler form. While I don't suggest women abandon their careers by the masses or toss their chili-pepper-red front-load washing machines by the wayside, I do encourage you to take inventory of where you expend your precious energy and how often you make time to refuel your limited reserves.

I recently finished reading *Gift from the Sea* by Ann Morrow Lindbergh, a highly acclaimed author of the twentieth century (not to mention the first female glider pilot in the U.S.,) whose accomplishments were overshadowed by her husband's notoriety.

In one resonant chapter, she speaks about the breakdown of the female spirit due to overwork. Keep in mind, this book was written back in the fifties. We've evolved five decades worth of new ways to overextend ourselves. She paints an interesting portrait of the exhausted spirit by cautioning readers against attempting to water a field instead of a garden with the reserves of one pitcher. I saw myself in that chapter. It was time to come clean.

I, Lucy Lemay Cellucci, being of sound(ish) mind and body, mother of two, wife of one, teacher, writer, artist, and barista, plead guilty to first-degree, premeditated pitcher-depletion.

I hereby accept my sentence: ninety days of porching.

On my porch, there are no plot arcs to craft. There are no lessons to plan. There are no customers to be served. There are no walls to be painted. There are no children needing my immediate attention. They're just on the other side of the door, draining what little sanity is left in their father. I admit I'm not above taking pleasure in this fact.

There is just me, sitting on my Adirondack chair with a cup of tea, surrounded by the flowers and shrubs in my garden. There are birds chirping nearby and the warm glow of the predusk sun, peeking out between tree branches as it begins its sleepy descent.

For one hour each evening, I take refuge on my concrete life-raft. It offers amnesty from the pace with which I have lived my life for the last five years. Here, I connect to the part of me that has the ability to be still. Here, I am not compelled to fill the silence with jokes or other inessential chatter. Here, I am simply living in the present, experiencing the joy of porching with a cup of chamomile tea on a lovely summer evening. (Okay, fine — sometimes it's a glass of wine — but only on special occasions, like the weekend or Tuesday.)

How grateful I am for this opportunity to temporarily detour off my racetrack and fill my long-emptied pitcher. I'm more thankful this much-needed respite happens during the summer months. Somehow I don't think my evenings spent porching would be so comforting mid-January. Occasionally, my son pokes his head out the door to observe my uncharacteristic inactivity.

"Mommy, are you looking at the sewers?" he asked me one night.

I looked up at him and smiled before I replied, "Yes, I am."

Thank you, Granny.

COFFEE BREAK

"Almost everything will work again if you unplug it for a few minutes ... including you."—Anne Lamott

Of all the memorable films to grace the screen in my living room, *American Beauty* is perhaps one of the most unforgettable. One of my favorite scenes occurs when Lester Burnham walks into a fast-food restaurant and politely asks for "the position with the least amount of responsibility."

This attitude was my inspiration between June 2011 and April 2013. During those years I hid from my career as a dance educator. Correction: I ran screaming for the hills, jumped off a cliff to fake my own death and assumed another identity as a partner at Starbucks. (*"Partner"* is the term Starbucks uses to define its employees and is nowhere near as provocative as it sounds.)

I was struck with how overwhelming it was to learn all the drinks. I actually brought in a journal to make some notes on my bar shifts ... something I'm sure was a source of amusement to my younger coworkers. Those damn caramel macchiatos always threw me off — I often forgot to pour the espresso shots last. Nor did I get the hang of the drinks at the cold bar. My apologies to anyone who received a smoothie made by me during the summer of 2011. I can recall with alarming accuracy my sense of panic as I watched the cups line up down the bar in my queue during "Frappy Hour." I felt like I was in that episode of *I Love Lucy* where she's a factory worker in charge of wrapping chocolates passing by on the conveyor belt — except stuffing all the missed drinks down my blouse to avoid my supervisor's disapproval wasn't an option for me. (Sorry to let you down, Annie. I really did try).

I still regard my time at Starbucks as my "extended vacation from work." That's precisely what it was; a break from being responsible for other people. For nearly two years, I got to have a job that required no previous planning prior to showing up, no phone calls to make, emails to send, endless searching for ideas, music or costumes. I wasn't responsible for anything outside of ensuring I showed up on time and providing courteous and reasonably competent service. The biggest bonus was that I got to be at home in the evenings to have dinner with my family, a rarity for many of us in the dance industry.

The most surprising thing about my stint at Starbucks was how I formed friendships with people who were at a completely different stage of life; most being a good decade (or two!) younger. After a couple of months, I was being invited to parties where beer pong and

Twister were played. We had a picnic in the park, a casino night, an evening at a comedy club, a romp at Laser Quest and a karaoke night. One of the most memorable evenings involved a birthday party honoring an intoxicated Latin-tongued partner who recited the works of Dr. Seuss to a delighted audience of co-workers. It appeared not much has changed in me since I was a younger adult, except my body hurts in the morning when I get out of bed. (I also require a lot more fiber in my diet, but you probably don't want to hear about that.)

 I also had the privilege of interacting with a rather cheeky partner who was in his seventies. Like me, this remarkable gentleman viewed his hours at the store as a break from his own challenges. Each weekday morning, he would check his "baggage" at the door and spend two hours smiling, singing, and pulling out the best parts of himself to make each customer feel personally acknowledged. To paraphrase him is embarrassingly inadequate since it does little to acknowledge the incredible strength, wisdom, and optimism this man possessed. Working alongside him left me both humbled and inspired by his courage. I remember the words he left us with at his retirement party: "*Just being alive means you're successful.*"

 The best part of my time at Starbucks wasn't the pride I felt when people looked at my gleaming pastry case (I actually miss cleaning that thing ... is that weird?) but how this job helped me sift through my depressive fog and reconnect with the ability to have fun. It gave me the time to stop and reflect on what was happening in my life, allowing me to see the areas where I needed to make some changes.

Change did find me. It started with the occasional appearance of Sarah Nolan, former dancer with the Royal Winnipeg Ballet and director of the Saskatchewan Contemporary Ballet. She had recently opened a dance studio in my neighborhood. She came to grab some goodies from my store one day and recognized me. On two separate occasions, she offered me a teaching position at her studio. On two separate occasions, I politely declined and instead offered to put whipped cream on her beverage. When the spring of 2013 arrived, I turned in my green apron and took some time off work to recover from the exhaustion that had accumulated since the birth of my second child. I found improved health, finished my manuscript and rediscovered I deeply missed being a dance teacher. Thankfully, I knew of a place where they were looking for one. Sarah welcomed me into her studio with open arms. Since that time, I have had the joy of reconnecting with other like-minded artistic spirits and finding my place among a new tribe. Sometimes, when we say "No, I can't," it really means "I'm just not ready right now."

My story ends on a more cheerful note than that of

my *American Beauty* counterpart. Lester Burnham never got to enjoy his newfound wisdom when the fog of his midlife crisis finally lifted. Since I have the good fortune to have neighbors who are kind enough not to shoot me, I can move forward with my healthier sense of self-awareness allowing me to construct my life in a way that works for me. I set firm boundaries of what I can handle not only as a teacher, but also a writer and a mother. I am one of those lucky people who gets to do what they love and loves what they do. I can't think of a more beautiful gift than knowing the life I'm living is a beautiful gift.

    Thanks for the coffee break, Starbucks.

THE GIFT OF PRESENCE

"Be happy in the moment, that's enough. Each moment is all we need, not more." — Mother Teresa

It's called presence because it is a gift that we may open in every moment when we bring to it our full attention. Be mindful of the disposition of young children; see the ease in their play. They do not occupy themselves with past regrets or future anxieties. They see only the vivid colors of flowers and insects, squealing with delight when their parents spray them with the garden hose.

See the acceptance of what is on the faces of those who understand they are on borrowed time. They do not put their energy into building investment portfolios or finishing home renovation projects. Instead, they bask in the company of the ones they love the most. Each moment is cherished as if it were a special occasion to be marked with candles and decorations.

Remove the filter of distraction from your experience. Leave the ongoing party of social media for a while. Our fear of what will happen in our absence is what removes us from being present.

If we could stop, look around and see that life is

happening in this moment rather than hiding in the next, waiting impatiently for us to complete our tasks, perhaps we would be inclined to show more kindness to one another. We wouldn't fret about the hours slipping into a new day, clutching wildly at them as we exert futile efforts to bend them to our will.

Position yourself to be open to the energy of others. Look people in the eye when you speak. Create joy through shared laughter. Make space to sit with someone in their pain. Hold them to you long enough so they feel comfort from your embrace.

Breathe in deeply. Taste food robustly. Feel gratitude often. Set aside your burdens and grievances to marvel at the fact that you have the privilege of struggle.

You, with all of your beauty and mess and terror and confusion push against your own magnificence, yet stubbornly cling to your claim on life. You are unaware the power of choice is yours to wield.

A heart is beating in your chest. The force that creates stars and planets has also created you. And you have the ability to draw into your orbit whatever satellites of pleasure you wish.

If only you would stop and take notice of what's happening right now.

      It's called presence because it is a gift.

CONCLUSION

"Happiness is not something you postpone for the future; it is something you design for the present."
—Jim Rohn

Something noticeable shifts inside of me after the second week in August. The evening light grows shorter and I find myself reaching for the long, three-quarter-length sweater in the hall closet to wrap around me those evenings spent outside. My leisurely strolls along the boardwalk of my favorite conservation area are replaced by rambling expeditions up and down department store aisles in search of school supplies.

The mornings spent at my laptop with my compositions are replaced by sketching out class plans and other teaching materials as my inevitable return to work creeps on the horizon.

What's truly impressive about all of this is how okay I am with it. As much as I adore the relaxed pace of summer with its lazy mornings of coffee on the deck, afternoons in the pool and late dinners enjoyed under a pink sky, my heart pledges allegiance to the autumn season. The cooler weather and warmer clothes, the sights, the smells, Thanksgiving, Halloween ... I love all of it. Autumn has an uncanny way of renewing my sense of wonder and optimism for life. It triggers a powerful nesting instinct. Was it a coincidence that both my children were born in the fall? I remember the weeks leading up to their births. I canned, pickled, baked and froze things to the point of mania. Even now, without preparing to welcome a new baby, I find myself returning to my kitchen. There is something incredibly comforting about coming into a house that's marinating in the aromas of culinary nurturing.

As a student, teacher, and parent, September has always been the beginning of the New Year. Oh sure, I give kisses and hugs at midnight on December 31st and wish everyone a "Happy New Year," but it's just a formality, merely my way of going with the flow and keeping a low profile.

September is the true harbinger of change.

This September, my resolve for a better year will not include counting my carbs, reading *Moby Dick,* nor learning to speak Mandarin. I will choose to direct my focus inward and build upon the things that reside inside of me that will bring about the kind of authentic happiness only I can provide for myself.

I attended a writer's workshop a few months back that taught writers how best to relate to their audience when writing nonfiction, to show how they, above anyone else, were qualified to write about their chosen topic. My qualifications for being a happiness writer include the impressive list of credentials below:

Zip.

Zilch.

Zero.

Oh, I almost forgot … sweet diddly squat.

If you got the impression while reading that I spent a Zen-like summer communing with nature, wound up with the big answers to life and returned to my kitchen to transfer my bliss into a batch of blueberry muffins then I have seriously misled you (I wonder if it's too late to get my money back from that workshop?)

I am just as much of a hot mess after writing this as I was before writing this. The biographical novel depicting my own life story would read less like *Eat, Pray, Love* and more like *Drink, Scream, Run*. I am about as close to having it all figured out as the scientific community is to proving string theory.

However, there is a ray of hope.

Did you ever play with a Rubik's Cube as a kid? Do you remember the feeling of pushing through your frustration, spending days or even weeks trying to get the colors to line up? One day, you got the green side together … you were so fired-up! You knew it wasn't really solved yet because the rest of the colors were still scattered but you could start to see that a pattern was evolving … you were on your way to understanding how it worked. You felt so good about yourself, you considered submitting a resume to NASA when you grew-up. You were reaching for those stars, baby. You knew all you had to do was hang in there and persevere. You had concrete proof of your ability to succeed.

This is where I am.

Shooting for the moon.

Landing among the stars.

I've got my greens together; solitude, gratitude, compassion, ease, and introspection. The biggest gift they've given me is this beautiful, lush space that holds my own joys, sorrows, and longings. The edges take root and sprawl out from the corners, pollinating the seeds of creativity, receptivity, and love. Being nourished in this way feeds my spirit and allows me to connect to a vital source of energy. I am sustained not only as an individual but also in my role to give and take with others.

The time has come for me to fold up the trail map, rely on my heart to be my compass and bring about a tidy conclusion to all things I've discussed in this book. But you know as well as I there are few tidy conclusions in life. What I have learned so far from my moments of solitude is real happiness is truly an inside job. I can hold no one accountable for it other than myself. If I'm serious about it, there are some housekeeping items I must continue to address. For your viewing pleasure, I will list them in bullet form. I'm told people like that sort of thing.

**I must consciously choose my thoughts for they govern my emotions, and in turn, my actions.

**I must release the need to hang onto things from the past that prevent me from moving forward.

**I need to keep myself focused on the blessings of what I have rather than what someone else has. The accomplishments of those around me are not indicative of my personal failings. They are evidence of what can happen when we crush our self-limiting beliefs and move towards our heart's desires.

**The greatest and most important love I have in my life is the relationship that I have with myself. The way I treat myself will overlap into my relationships with others making me a better wife, mother, sister, daughter, teacher, and friend. This means I should work diligently at showing myself kindness. It is of no benefit to anyone for me to slide into a harness and plow the field as if I were a Clydesdale. Aligning myself with the practices of self-care will do more for everyone I care about than keeping my head down and constantly taking one for the team. It goes without saying that coffee and wine should never be considered a viable substitution for a good night's sleep. Marriage is difficult. I don't need to make it more difficult by cultivating an attitude of entitlement over how I should be loved. Loving somebody in a long-term and satisfying way requires sustained effort on what you are giving to the relationship. If I am no longer able to show up for my part of this effort, I must examine why that is and not lay that responsibility at my husband's feet. Otherwise, my experience in the relationship will be one of pain and frustration.

**My children are not extensions of me and should not be treated as such. They are here to write their own stories and my role, as they age, is to give them the freedom to create their own narratives. The idea of relinquishing control is an uncomfortable prospect for many of us.

**It is a lot easier to achieve when we are not pursuing accomplishments through our children. When we make our contentment contingent upon their behavior, we set ourselves up for failure. *

Lastly, and perhaps most important: take a breath. If I have any hope of bringing peace and contentment into my life, I must be willing to sit and be still. I must allow stillness to approach me and listen to what it has to say, which is counterintuitive to those biological instincts I have been given as a human. I must stop looking outside of myself to chase after happiness, clubbing it over the head and dragging it back to my cave.

Oftentimes it can only be through giving up the search that we find what we are looking for. It really is a beautiful story unfolding around me; now all I have to do is let it in. Hopefully in some way you are doing the same with your story. Experience all your narratives have to offer, embrace your plot twists, feel gratitude for your character developments and take the time to remind yourself to live fully in each page. Feeling whole and happy isn't something that is waiting for you over there. It's with you right now. It's been with you the whole time. You don't need to wait any longer. You don't need to have more love, money, accolades, or followers.

You just need to stop and notice what experiences you are creating.

Sit still and pay attention to what your heart is telling you. Do you hear it?

You are loved.

You are enough.

You are here.

Lucy Lemay Cellucci is a Canadian author who first began her storytelling career in northern Ontario, crafting tales of creative fiction when her high school theatre teacher would inquire, often in front of the entire class, the reason for her habitually late arrivals. Her ability to weave tales that evoked laughter from her peers and irritated teacher was her earliest lesson in the power of storytelling to shift human emotions.

An avid outdoor enthusiast, Lucy spends as much time as she can in the picturesque conservation areas that surround her Ottawa, Ontario home, providing her with the cradle of inspiration and solitude needed for her creative pursuits.

She can be reached at:

Email --- Author@lucylcellucci.net

Facebook---https://www.facebook.com/authorllc

Instagram---www.instagram.com/thestorytellerllc

Or at www.thestorytellerspage.com

Made in the USA
Middletown, DE
18 November 2019